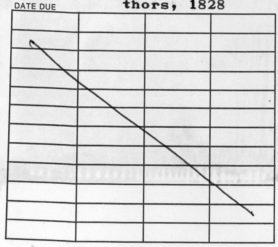

SKETCHES OF

CONTEMPORARY AUTHORS, 1828

Frederick Denison Maurice

SKETCHES OF
CONTEMPORARY AUTHORS, 1828

by

FREDERICK DENISON MAURICE

A. J. Hartley, editor

Archon Books
1970

SBN: 208 00904 3

Library of Congress Catalog Card Number: 74-106555

PRINTED IN THE UNITED STATES OF AMERICA

CONTENTS

Preface   vii

Acknowledgements   ix

Introduction   xi

English Literature   1

Mr. Jeffrey and the Edinburgh Review   6

Mr. Southey   12

Mr. Cobbett   22

Mr. Wordsworth   33

Mr. Moore   44

Mr. Brougham   54

Percy Bysshe Shelley   66

Sir Walter Scott   76

Sir James Mackintosh   91

Maria Edgeworth   99

Lord Byron   110

Mr. James Mill   117

Appendices   131

Index   150

ACKNOWLEDGEMENTS

I record my thanks to the Canada Council, whose generous assistance made a first assessment of *Sketches* possible; to the Committee on Research at McGill University for further assistance; and to the Faculty of Graduate Studies at Dalhousie University, for support in the form of a Summer Research Grant and assistance in the final preparation of the manuscript.

I wish, further, to express my gratitude to all who, in one way and another, gave personal aid; particularly, to the young Graduate who, like Maurice, admires Coleridge so much; and, lastly, to the ingenious detective, whose "golden deeds" inform more than one footnote.

I also thank the editor and publisher for their permission to quote from *The Kingdom of Christ,* edited by Alec R. Vidler (2 vols., SCM Press, 1958).

NOTE

In the interests of the reader, I have normalised Maurice's use of capitals, punctuation, and spelling, and I have divided his longer paragraphs, some of which ran into several pages of unbroken print. Otherwise, with the exception of minor stylistic changes inherent in the transfer from periodical to book format, the text is that printed in the *Athenaeum* (January – June, 1828).

PREFACE

Though Maurice's critical *Sketches* include no essay on Coleridge, they are Coleridgean in tone and spirit. Broadly appropriating an organic critical theory, Maurice in 1828 was content to saturate each essay with Coleridge's Christian (social) philosophy, the knowledge and use of which were vital, both believed, for valid literary craftsmanship, whether critical or creative. Like the poets of the period, Maurice derived inspiration from Coleridge and, though he ultimately applied to theology what they incorporated into poetry, they in turn were not infrequently influenced by his feeling for Coleridge, whose writings united them in a common aim, a consuming desire to make the world better.

Having established the relation between literature and society in his introductory remarks, Maurice begins the series proper with essays on the literature of criticism — albeit prejudiced — as represented by Jeffrey and Southey. To follow are his sketches on creative authors. Shelley, for example, is revealed in a halo of imagination as an author of the highest order, while Scott, who is caught in the trammels of fancy, becomes inevitably a writer of lower rank. Byron, as one who betrayed his imagination, perverted his prophetic task. There are also essays on James Mill and Sir James Mackintosh whose works, though logical and instructive, are confined by an understanding devoid both of feeling and of imaginative understanding.

Collected in one volume, which, it is hoped, may be useful as a handbook of comments on romantic theory and terminology, these essays irradiate the romantic period. The introductory essay, in addition to placing *Sketches* in historical and biographical perspective, attempts to explain Maurice's views on the nature of language as a primal force in shaping society. It is but one of several themes worthy of exploration and, though derived from Coleridge, it gains much by Maurice's interpretative application to the writings of some of his more notable contemporaries.

To see these *Sketches* through the eyes of Maurice, then a

young critic possessed of the belief that poetics and morality grow together, is to see the romantic movement vividly and in breadth. It is also to see some of the principal figures in it in confrontation, less with one another and with the issues of the day, than as prophets proceeding against the stream of established complacency inevitably to usher in a new day.

A. J. H.

Dalhousie University
June, 1969

Introduction

The *Athenaeum* and John Frederick Denison Maurice began their careers together. The periodical was launched as a literary and critical journal in January 1828, and with the publication of the third number on January 16 appeared the introduction to Maurice's series of essays on contemporary writers. As an introductory piece, it suggests something of the aims of his series, the principles tempering his views, and the authors he intends to review. Though the essays are not precisely concurrent with the weekly publication of the periodical, the series of *Sketches* — twelve critical commentaries in addition to the introductory piece — had appeared by June 18, and it is clear that Maurice wished them to be regarded as a whole.[1] Each *Sketch,* treating a single writer as it does, is complete in itself, but the essays give as well a picture of the "wondrous regeneration" which, as Maurice saw, marked the beginning of a new era in literature.

Each essay is precisely what a sketch should be — a brief account conveying general ideas, but without great detail. Assuming generalisations to arise from a ground of principle and conviction, Maurice believed them to reveal and enlarge thought. He felt that an author should be judged by the "general impression" of his works. More than a generation before Matthew Arnold, he had insisted that a critic ought himself to be possessed of "the best that is known and thought in the world" in order to "propagate" it for others in his own writings. Maurice, like other nineteenth-century thinkers, regarded the acquisition of knowledge as an organic growth, and generalisation was one way in which thought might be made to expand like a plant growing from the soil of known truths. The *Sketches* thus relate the thought of each author to that of all the others considered in the series, and together they illuminate the romantic period.

During the indecisive period between his leaving Cambridge in

---

[1] The Cambridge Apostles supplied all the copy for the *Athenaeum* at this point, the Rev. Henry Stebbing and Maurice editing as well. See *The Life of Frederick Denison Maurice,* edited by Frederick Maurice (2 vols., 1884), i, 78, the source of the biographical and historical data in this introduction.

1827 and his going up to Oxford in 1830, Maurice had wavered between Law and Literature. At Cambridge he had become a member of a literary society, the Apostles Club; and before he left the university he was the acknowledged leader of this intellectual body of men. Throughout most of 1826 he and a friend, Charles Whitmore,[2] had jointly edited the *Metropolitan Quarterly Magazine,* to which the Apostles and other undergraduates had contributed. The magazine was too hostile to the existing order to last long, but its brief life nevertheless showed the wish of the Apostles to reform the world, and they thought this could be done by the pen. When in 1827 Maurice and John Sterling went up to London with literary work in mind, and when in the Peace Society James Silk Buckingham learned through Maurice's father of their literary interests, he engaged the young men to fill the columns of his newly established *Athenaeum.* In addition, each of them — Whitmore, Sterling, and Maurice — began a novel.

That the *Athenaeum* did not pay, that Maurice's connection with it terminated with the writing of the article on James Mill (June 18), that he became editor of the *Literary Chronicle* only to see it merge almost at once with the *Athenaeum,* are happenings by the way. By June, 1829, when he had quenched his youthful ardour for topical writing and had seen the chasms separating great authorship from periodical anonymity, he had resolved to take holy orders, and to that end he had arranged to enter Exeter College, Oxford.

Ordained in 1834, he meant not to abandon letters, but to bring to English literature a deeper knowledge of its Christian heritage, an aim which he pursued admirably for thirteen years as Professor of English Literature and Modern History at King's College, London. But he had already done this, though more inadvertently, in his *Sketches of Contemporary Authors.*

Though Maurice wrote voluminously throughout his career, he had expressed the full range of his thought by 1840 with the publication in the *Encyclopaedia Metropolitana* of his long outline on moral and metaphysical philosophy, a work which, from that time until the close of his life in 1872, he intermittingly expanded into two large volumes. *Moral and Metaphysical Philosophy* and *The Kingdom of Christ,* which had appeared in 1838, contain his principal ideas. These ideas were in part formulated by 1828, and the writing of the *Sketches* helped him to bring

[2] Charles Shapland Whitmore (1806-77).

them into focus.

At twenty-three, Maurice was considerably younger than his "contemporaries". Jeffrey, for instance, was fifty-five; Scott, fifty-seven; and Wordsworth, fifty-eight. In these *Sketches* Maurice, though earnest and reserved, has expressed himself with the exuberance of a young graduate. To have declared James Mill's philosophy, for example, to make "truth and benevolence mere instruments for supporting those wants which we have in common with the brutes", was to express a firm conviction. At the same time, it placed Maurice, a romantic in a romantic age, firmly among the Coleridgeans. The ideas thus expressed in the *Sketches* are those of Christian Platonism, and the critical theme in all of them is that the great majority of men in his generation, as in most, have mistaken the shadow of truth for truth itself.

Always of a theological turn of mind, Maurice had begun to think in terms of the concept of *Christus Consummator*.[3] He began at the beginning with God, for His Kingdom had existed from the beginning and would exist for ever. That meant, logically, that it exists in the *here* and the *now* and, though it exists in heaven, it must also absorb the whole of life on earth while at the same time remaining indivisible from its heavenly counterpart. Had not Christ established the Kingdom of God upon earth?

Maurice saw that men might experience the Kingdom in various ways. First of all, it exists within each of us. This meant, therefore, that it must also thrive and grow in the social body, of which the family is the nucleus, and which inevitably expands into the community and the nation. The Kingdom of God lives in human relationships and in the invisible relationships between man and God.

For Maurice, the Kingdom in the heart of a man is the very being of the man. Though man is of earth, the life which he has but which is not his, is a gift of God whence it came. Theologically speaking, Maurice spoke of this vital life as the conscience. Everywhere throughout his writings he was to speak of the conscience as a "feeling", a "teacher", a "light". The conscience is illuminated by the "divine Word": God informs it; or, very simply, it may be said that Being informs the human being.

The conscience is also seen as something in a man saying "I ought or I ought not", and in his relationships with society a man

---

[3]The concept arose in Maurice's novel, *Eustace Conway*, begun in 1828 and published in three volumes in 1834, and was developed in *The Kingdom of Christ*, recently reprinted from the second edition, 1842, edited by Alec R. Vidler (2 vols., 1958). See *The Life of Maurice*, i, 167.

knows whether he "ought" or "ought not". He has freedom to choose. Though good must conquer at last, man has a natural tendency to say he "ought" when he knows he "ought not."[4] Good and evil therefore exist, and it is Maurice's contention that every moral principle has its "attendant counterfeit".[5] By means of a reconciliation between these opposing tendencies, the earthly kingdom exists in a state of becoming. In the process of becoming men of good will struggle unceasingly to reconcile evil with good; and again, Being is the helper in the struggle. But man is essentially moral.

Morever, the conscience can reveal its choice only in action. A feeling belonging to the eternal, the conscience in action is "the most intense sense of a vocation to help and instruct others". Man must choose, but since he can only "live" for others, he is social as well as moral. Again, though leaving him free to choose, Being directs human being.

Uniquely, however, in Maurice's theology language plays an important part. In writing sketches of contemporaries whose work he chose to assess, Maurice's attention was directed to the mystical nature of language and its equally mystical synthesis in literature. Steeped in Coleridge's thought, Maurice conceived the conscience to be what Coleridge claimed it to be – an "experience *sui generis*", or a "testifying state" arising from the "coincidence of the human will with reason and religion".[6] A "testifying state" implies a medium through which reason and will under the guidance of God may "testify", and this medium is of necessity language. Language is thus seen to be the only interpreter of conscience, so that conscience and language become inter-dependent. In Coleridge's, as well as Maurice's view, language and conscience, as well as being mutually inter-dependent, emanate from the same Source, variously termed God, Being, or the Word. Language is therefore prior to man: when Being informed being the Word already was, and gave human being the word. Man is a moral and social creature: he is so because of

---

[4] A recurrent theme in *Eustace Conway,* ultimately clarified in nine lectures on casuistry published as *The Conscience* (1868). Maurice also discussed it in his long article, "Moral and Metaphysical Philosophy", *The Encyclopaedia Metropolitana* (1839), ii, 580, 648 (hereafter, MM.).

[5] MM., ii, 673, with a fuller discussion in his famous *Theological Essays* (1853), recently reprinted with an introduction by Edward Carpenter (1957), p. 278.

[6] S. T. Coleridge, *Lay Sermons* (3rd. ed., 1853), pp. 19, 70-73.

language: he remains so by means of language.

Language, therefore, is "the sign and organ of humanity".[7] If on the one hand language relates man to God, on the other it separates him from the beasts. Language renders human communication possible. Essentially moral, however, man must choose his mode of communication. If he is linguistically responsible he is "the mouthpiece of Being". If he is linguistically irresponsible he denies his own conscience and the Being who gave it to him, and builds his own Babel. He is authentically man, however, only when he is true to the Kingdom within and his words thus contribute to the building of the Kingdom without.

Social forms and institutions pre-suppose language and, thus seen, the literature of a nation is the soul of that nation, filling every part of its being. Maurice was later to affirm more explicitly a theme assumed in these essays, that the nation and its literature in the first instance arise together, both acquiring unity and coherence with the accomplishment of an adequate and cohesive language. The *Sketches* also take it for granted that literature is greatest when political unity in the nation is most fully realized, and when each man, while subscribing himself to the nation, is yet aware of his dignity as a person and accepts the voice of the nation as his own.[8]

The interest in words had been stimulated in the Apostles Club. With men like Richard Chenevix Trench, Maurice was among the first of nineteenth-century thinkers to revive an interest in the nature of language. He saw that words are alive and vital. Thought, whether the noblest of which man is capable or the meanest to which he may sink, lies stone dead until enlivened and borne upward on the wing of the word. Like the wind in Shelley's Ode, words

>Drive . . . dead thought over the universe
>Like withered leaves to quicken a new birth!

The word is the greatest power our world knows, and its potential is both terrible and terrifying.

Moreover, the poet's words — those of any responsible writ-

---

[7]Maurice, *Subscription No Bondage* (1835), pp. 46-7.

[8]MM., ii, 557, but developed in the lectures assembled and prefaced by Thomas Hughes as *The Friendship of Books* (1874), p. 141

er — are not "mere words". They are events, creating new historical situations. Maurice criticised Scott for showing us only the
pageant of history, thus administering, Maurice thought, only to
a "craving for mere amusement", whereas genuine history must
show, not merely what the world was, but the means available in
a given epoch for its general improvement. Feelings alone indicate the spirit of a time, and thus the designs taking shape within
it. Men act upon their understanding of words; and men, like
words themselves, are instruments of morality. The Christian interpretation of history is that words, echoing the Incarnate Word,
were spoken, and that actual events occurred as a result of
them.[9] Maurice felt that authors should use words in this spirit.

Critics, he insisted, need to respect the words of an author,
who can be understood only on his own terms. It is easy to be
subjective, but the business of the critic is to interpret a work
objectively in terms of what the author actually meant in the
context in which he wrote. The critic must assist the author in
his effort to be understood. It was precisely for this conscience-
less or irresponsible use of words that Maurice attacked Francis
Jeffrey, editor of the *Edinburgh,* and others like Southey, who
wrote for the *Quarterly.*

In Maurice's thought, inspiration differs not at all from conscience, for both are informed from without, and are valid to the
degree that the creature hears and obeys a Voice. Both conscience and inspiration operate in action, and operate for good
only when both remain moral, conscience informing the will to
act, and inspiration, the genius to create. The poet must "battle"
for the regeneration of man. "The poet and the prophet are the
true priests of mankind; for through them the word of Being is
mediated".[10] According to the light of his peculiar genius, the
critic, however, is not debarred from assisting at the altar of
learning. But he must be "responsible".

During the first six months of 1828 while Maurice was writing
these essays, Waterloo was but a dozen years in the past and the
Reform Bill but four in the future. As Maurice said, men's minds
were "all afloat", but in 1828 England was nevertheless entering
upon a new era. As Shakespeare was to the Renaissance, so the

[9]MM., ii, 558, 630-31. See *What is Revelation* (1859), p. 54, and *The Friendship of Books,* pp. 57-60.

[10]Alan Richardson, "When is a Word an Event?", *The Listener,* LXXIII (3 June 1965), p. 819.

romantic poets were the "second miraculous descent upon English literature of the purifying and kindling fire from heaven". Here, at a height of national power, there occurred a fresh outburst of poetry. Here, in Maurice's own youth, was the proof of his thesis on the nature of language. The poets of the time, seemingly under the influence of an "extraordinary afflatus",[11] informed their words with an imaginative radiance that enabled them to create a soul for the living body of the nation: here were Wordsworth and Coleridge; Byron, Shelley, and Keats. Here, as his contemporaries, were poets fit to image the nation at the height of her glory.

In Maurice's view, the great romantic poets, Byron excepted, were all responsible poets whose poetry was "the spontaneous outgrowth" of their minds. They reflected "all feelings" but cherished only "the best". Possessing the fundamental quality of "innate goodness", they endeavoured to develop it in their writings. All were gifted with "inward universality". Owing to their awareness of God's presence all were ennobled to instruct mankind in the eternal principles which alone can uplift and inspire the whole mass of society. They could testify outwardly for God because inwardly they knew and obeyed His Voice.

More intensely than other poets of the period, Wordsworth seemed to Maurice the recipient of a "kindling fire" from heaven. Through the medium of a "faithful and fertile imagination" Wordsworth saw the spirit of good permeating all mankind and reflected in all nature around him. With rare insight he transmuted this goodness and beauty into permanent poetic forms. Shelley, too, was guided by a "pillar of fire". He, too, worked from invisible principles. He saw "the essence of good" as a Spirit. He separated good from evil and brought goodness and light into "a focus of unmingled love". "Absorbed and transfigured into poetry", Shelley achieved a "perfect unity of feeling" for the cultivation and improvement of mankind.

All writers, however, are not poets and prophets. Moreover, there are good and bad poets, true and false prophets, and critics who are irresponsible. Writers may carelessly pervert semantic values. They may, by employing weak words, rush their readers past reality after reality. They may use words that, far from quickening "a new birth", deaden feelings by attempting to sustain a fixed and mouldering past. They may employ them menda-

---

[11] *Theological Essays*, p. 228.

ciously in an effort to destroy all that human tradition has held
to be true. They may attempt, in the teeth of Providence, to set
up their own systems for the operation and government of the
world instead of accepting God's scheme which already exists as
the foundation of the universe.

Of the twelve authors reviewed in the *Sketches* several of them
belong to that distinct class of writer known as the periodical
essayist and, as we have seen, that man was a power to be reck-
oned with. What kind of power did the periodical essayist wield,
Maurice asked? Did the critic speak through a conscience illuminated by the Word? Did he testify as the result of an "experience" representing the coincidence of will, reason, and religion?
As critical readers, the reviewers frequently made it their business
to read, not in terms of what the writer actually meant in the
context in which he had written, but in terms of an expedient
suited to their particular needs at the moment. Equally clearly,
critics read in this way quite deliberately. They used words, not
for moral purposes, not as a hopeful contribution to the building
of the Kingdom, but for the transient applause of a public whose
opinions they had largely shaped.

The *Athenaeum* had been founded as a "paper of principle",
and the Apostles who initiated it had laid down principles[1 2] —
"fixed rules" — to which they referred their compositions. Ideal-
istically, they had planned that the *Athenaeum* should be "the
resort of the most distinguished philosophers, historians, orators,
and poets" of the day, and they had hoped that these distinguished men might themselves be "proud of the records of their
fame" as preserved in the journal. As these *Sketches* show, Maurice, whether criticising poets like Wordsworth and Shelley, or
reviewers like Jeffrey, applied to all of them the same criteria of
judgment.

Though doubtless in agreement with the "fixed rules" of composition, his criteria clearly arose from his conclusions about the
fundamental nature of language — that it is a human medium
through which, under guidance from without, reason and will
unite within in an outward expression of human being, testifying
that the being is moral and social and, through the essential
historicity of language itself, eternal as well. For Maurice, an
author's work must not rest in particular phenomena, for these,
as Plato taught, are but manifestations of universal truth. "Great

[1 2] L. A. Marchand, *The Athenaeum Mirror of Victorian Culture* (1941), pp. 1, 10.

thinkers express wide principles in few words". Everywhere in
these *Sketches,* too, Maurice applauded authors who saw men,
not as members of parties and sects, but as "partakers of a common humanity". Maurice's sensitivity to the writer's compassion
for "common humanity" foreshadowed the Christian Socialist
movement, which he and J. F. M. Ludlow were to inaugurate in
1848. Again, as a romantic showing us romanticism from the
inside, he employed the Coleridgean distinction between Fancy
and Imagination to show his readers that those authors who, in
his view, contributed little of permanent worth, were lacking in
that first requisite of the true poet, Imagination. All these criteria
led Maurice to judgments which, though frequently counter to
those of his contemporaries, have been confirmed by posterity.

In Maurice's view, the reviewers under consideration deadened
men's feelings, spread confusion, and promoted chaos. They
damaged the soul of the nation. Though England stood at the
height of empire, though a body of poet-prophets under inspiration mirrored and exalted that nation, here was the "attendant
counterfeit". The word was often uttered in disobedience, and
with the word so perverted the nation must fall a prey to corruption. The word could be used in the service of life, or it could be
made an agent of death. Under conscience, these men had chosen. Did Maurice in 1828 have a premonition, one wonders, that
in 1853 he was to be cut off from his professorships (theological
as well as literary) in King's College by the wilful distortions and
mutilations of his work in the hands of reviewers who, wise in
their generation, sought public applause?

In the *Sketches* Maurice discriminated between truth and falsehood, between the classical and the ephemeral. The poet — the
responsible writer — helps the reader to *experience* "states of
feeling" so that he may apprehend "thought coloured by feeling".[13] Uplifting the mind, he leads on to "universal harmony",
while the critic aggravates division and dissent. While Southey
struggled with his "fretful load of prejudices" and Cobbett
barked with the "hounds of faction" — while periodical essayists
puffed their way across the contemporary stage — Wordsworth
quietly informed the time with "the breath of universal existence" and Shelley irradiated it with "imaginative splendour".
Poets, using words with care and veneration, teach universal
truths and build the Kingdom, but sophists, whose momentary

---

[13] J. S. Mill's familiar but significant phrases from *Autobiography* (1924), p. 125.

glitter is past, lie dead and forgotten, their kingdoms in dust.

Maurice was not suggesting that all poets are good, all reviewers bad. But in the application of his criteria of judgement the critics were found to betray themselves to ephemeral expedients, wilfully to harm others and, ultimately, the whole nation, for their own selfish ends. But as Byron scorned a humanity that would not applaud him and was therefore a perverted poet contributing nothing to the Kingdom, so Brougham was, on the whole, a useful if ephemeral orator, advocate, and essayist; and poet-essayist as he was, Southey did much for human regeneration until he sank into petty sectarianism. And Jeffrey's "liveliness, prettiness, and neatness of mind, were brought into full play by their corresponding qualities in the object of his admiration," namely Thomas Moore.

Traditionally, the poet and prophet (preacher and teacher) had been the priests of mankind. Now, a third voice, that of the periodical essayist, had arisen to direct thought. These men had proclaimed themselves mouthpieces for the nation; presumably, therefore, they were "linguistically responsible". But serious men like Maurice were troubled in the concurrence of two fundamental thoughts: the *essential* morality of the human being, and the power of his words. In the mouths of these men, that power was terrifying indeed. Maurice was heavily underlining the invisible but intense struggle at the core of both individual and national being.

In the imperial England of 1828 the seeds of self-destruction were being sown. The responsible writer, the poet-prophet, saw; and seeing, he soared to the refuge of the Ideal. What, indeed, was their reach for the unattainable but a lamentation for their world turning from its heaven, for their people wandering from their God? What, at last, was the voice of Keats's nightingale but the voice of the poet-prophet himself, painfully aware that his voice must "fade" at last "on the foam/ Of perilous seas" of irresponsible and meaningless jargon?

Maurice has suggested good and evil at work in the literature of his time. Everywhere in his essays he applauded schemes for the amelioration of the people, but he insisted that any improvement, to be genuine, must nurture the mind as well as the body. Democracy must follow in the wake of reform. But unless the rising democracy were grounded on the foundation of things, it would inevitably develop into one of two states, either of which, by the very nature of the case, must exist uncertainly and largely void of truth: without the Word,[14] the nation would become either a competitive stock exchange or a communist proletariat. In the former, loveless individuals must struggle to their deaths; in the latter, the individual loses himself in the herd. From the lyrical and ideal rhapsodist to the practical and mundane essayist the choice between linguistic responsibility and linguistic irresponsibility lay in the literature of the day. Like Blake, Maurice admonished the reader of his essays to "hear the voice of the bard!"

[14]The consequences for humanity "without the Word" are tremendous. They are startlingly stated in Maurice, "Dialogue between Somebody ... and Nobody", *Tracts on Christian Socialism* (1850), I, 8. See *The Life of Maurice,* ii, 8.

SKETCH I

English Literature[1]

There are some people who believe our age so infinitely the most important the world has ever known, that their opinions and boastings might well put us in mind of Voltaire's *un homme tel que moi*. It is after the fashion of that worthy's remarks on his own dignity that we constantly hear the present century applauded by its minions; and half the speeches at county dinners, and leading articles in daily newspapers, are filled with ejaculations in the name of the nineteenth century – *un siècle tel que moi*.[2]

There are others whose interest leads them to laud the wisdom of our ancestors as something altogether super-human. But these are not the only persons who cast longing looks behind them, and who delight to lose the present among the shadowy mazes of a far antiquity. The gradual deterioration of the world and its inhabitants was a favourite theory with an elder generation than ours; and while we feel all the inconveniences of the passing hour and turn our eyes only to the treasures, and glories, and prominent lights of antiquity, it is not very wonderful that we are somewhat inclined to prefer the historical to the actual and to take refuge in fancy, from our personal annoyances, amid the calm and lofty deliciousness of the by-gone day.

Both parties are probably mistaken. The same capacities exist at all times among men; but there certainly never has been a state of society which would permit the development of those capacities in anything like the perfection which they are destined to

[1] *Athenaeum* (16 January 1828).

[2] Believing that an epoch, like a man, has a characteristic individuality, Maurice uses Voltaire to establish the background of his own time. As a Frenchman equally at home in England, Prussia, and Switzerland, Voltaire represents Europe; and as dramatist, poet, and historian, "the intellectual king of the century", he also symbolises literary breadth and excellence. But above all, as a disciple of Locke and Newton he stands for liberality and reform, recurrent themes in these *Sketches*. The "man", boastful but peerless, was the progenitor of the "century" in which Maurice's contemporaries wrote.

arrive at hereafter. Our own time has reached, in everything connected with the senses, a degree of excellence which probably was not foreseen by any ancient philosopher. The powers of matter have been explored and applied in a thousand varieties of ways which, convenient, interesting, and beautiful as they are, yet seem to be only an early step in an illimitable progression. It may be doubted, however, whether we have advanced at all proportionably in those higher and interior qualities which are of infinitely more importance towards the perfection of each individual nature, but display themselves far less definitely by outward and calculable manifestations.[3]

Whatsoever may be the mechanical advantages or the social condition of a people, the same mighty principles of moral advancement, the same germs of truth and love, though often slumbering and torpid, yet live eternally in the hearts of the people. A large portion of this innate good has uniformly been developed among the greatest writers of every country.[4] It is one of the primary elements of genius and, perhaps, the most essential. To trace its appearance in the literature of any land or period, and to examine the mode in which it has moulded and assimilated to itself the forms which are the outgrowth and characteristic peculiarities of the people and the time, is an efficacious and delightful mode of throwing out into vigorous exertion the most precious qualities of our own minds.

But to search in this way into the most remarkable intellects of our own day and country and to know, with a learned spirit, the qualities of the masters of our generation, bears with it a more direct and obvious benefit; for though it be perfectly certain that the man of the highest genius is he in whom there is most of the eternal and the universal, of those qualities which are independent of climates and centuries, and government and education, which lend their power to the forms through which they show themselves, instead of resting on those forms for their success; yet it is also certain that when genius has breathed into these lifeless shapes and idols the breath of its nostrils, they assume a reality and seem to move with an independent life, whereby we learn more of their origin and purport than from a thousand minute delineations of details and peculiarities not informed by this inspiration. The man, moreover, of the mighti-

[3]Materially advanced in 1828, the epoch must now grow in wisdom.

[4]Men of genius, great writers, nurture man's moral nature.

est energies and sympathies will uniformly imbue with his own mind and rule, for his own purposes, all that is merely formal and accidental in the state of things to which he belongs.[5] He will not reject the aid of the implements which are scattered round him; but he will wield them to his own purposes and with a power unknown to those whose hands first shaped and employed them; and thus it is that in studying the minds and works of great writers we arrive at a deeper and more living knowledge of the epoch to which we belong, than if we looked, however widely, over its surface, or mined, however long and darkly, in its inmost caves. It is, moreover, in the writings of such men that we arrive at the most precise acquaintance with the general and permanent causes which, even around our daily paths, are moulding and inspiring the whole mass of that society whereof ourselves are portions.

There is much, also, to be learned from the examination even of those inferior, though still in some degree remarkable men, who often enjoy for a season a larger share of popularity and vulgar applause than wiser and more pregnant intellects. But in every study of this kind, the great point to be kept in view is this: viz. that the examination of individual character, as well as every other species of human research, is only valuable inasmuch as it assists the workings of the spirit of truth within us. The light pursuits of the most frivolous, the elaborate inquiries of cumbrous erudition, the experiments of the man of science, the perils and labours of the pilgrims of knowledge, all are equally contemptible and worthless except as assistances towards the nourishing into consciousness those general principles, the obscure records of wisdom, the lines of eternal truth, originally traced upon our minds, however faint and dim, by the hand of Him who is at once all wisdom and all truth. Of this knowledge, after the secrets of our own being have become manifest to our eyes, it is most important to us, as agents and instruments of good, to become acquainted with the state of custom, and feeling, and thought, among those around us.

To every portion of mankind, to every age, has been assigned its peculiar character. There are national as well as individual idiosyncrasies; and different races are no less distinguished by the variety of their arms and dresses — the Roman sword, the Gothic lance, the Indian tomahawk — than by the distinctive features of

---

[5]Men of genius distinguish the accidental and the transient from the eternal.

their customs, opinions, and modes of feeling. We catch a glimpse of human society shadowed afar off among the dim outlines of tents and camels, and the flocks of patriarchs, and the palm-trees of Arabia. The stamp of conquest and the records of priestly tyranny are exhibited, broad and deep, among the fearful gradations of castes, the stupendous monuments and pretended theocracy of Egypt, Etruria, and Hindustan. The very name of Greece calls up the image of the sunlit city with the music, the dances, the pageants, and the songs of its theatres; the perfection of human vigour displayed in the palaestra in shapes of an almost ideal beauty; the temples and the statues, the lovely phantasms of a poetical religion; the impassioned throng around the bema of the orator, and the eloquent meditations of a noble philosophy. The grave and simple unity of Roman forms, which made the city a camp, and the camp a temple, the lictors and the curule chair — the outward dress of a system in which everything was included under positive institutions, are no less distinct from the barbaric magnificence and startling contrasts of the fiery East, than from the rough, unorganized energy of the Teutonic tribes, the forest domain, the herds and huts, the irregular council and naked array of the Hercynian wilderness.[6] Again, another era presents to us the very busy marts of Bruges, and the crowded manufactories of Florence; the innumerable fortresses of feudal Germany with their buttresses of rock and their men of iron; the tribunals of love, the troubadours and jongleurs, in the palaces of Thoulouse; the astrolabe and sigil, the tournament and bull-fight of Granada; with the horrible extravagances of crusades, and the elaborate follies of scholastic logic.

It may seem to some the result of a severe wisdom to say that these are all recollections striking indeed to the fancy, for this at least will be allowed by everyone, but without the slightest pretension to any substantial value. Yet these things are all symptoms of the particular forms under which human nature subsisted at certain epochs, and in various modes of society. These epochs and modes of national existence were each of them as marked in their own individual being as are single men.

This is very remarkably true of the present age of European society. The latter portion of the eighteenth century was the beginning of a new era, which is even yet but in its earlier

[6]The wooded mountain system of middle Germany and northern Austria.

stages.[7] It is difficult to form even a faint and vague conception of the mighty events and incalculable revolutions which its progress is destined to unfold. Who is there who can venture to affirm that we ourselves shall not be the spectators of changes more startling, widely-spreading, and permanently important than all the shatterings of thrones, the convulsions of governments, the earthquake shocks of universal opinion, or even than that wondrous regeneration of literature which has so suddenly begun to enlarge the prospects of mankind, and has so astounded the exclusive worshippers of the dead and mouldering past?

We can foresee little of the future; but still we can see something: and we should be madmen or idiots to close our eyes and shut up the volumes of divination, while that great movement is bearing onward the whole world by which we, too, must be swept along. The signs of the times are around us, many and various, and prominent; but we find them, above all, in the writings of those men, some of whom are even now so powerfully influencing society, while others are treasures reserved and hoarded up for the benefit of, perhaps, a distant futurity. We therefore propose to examine those minds of our own day which are the most conspicuous in literature for good or for evil;[8] and though we are well aware that we can employ but very inadequate means, yet we hope we may venture to assert that our pen will be guided by no feeling but the free love of truth.

[7]Though the "signs of the times" are to be read in the writings of the authors under review, Maurice places them in perspective: the "new era", its ends unknown, had its beginnings in the empiricism of the eighteenth century.

[8]As a critic, Maurice will distinguish the man of genius, the poet-prophet who "enlarges the prospects of mankind", from the literary theorist and demagogue.

SKETCH II

Mr. Jeffrey and the *Edinburgh Review*[1]

The *Edinburgh Review* is now chiefly known as a political pamphlet of great talent published once a quarter. The gold and azure of its dawning gives us the promise of three or four solid calculating articles on history and political economy, a paper of pleasant jokes against the Tories and, perhaps, a few pages of scandalous chronicle on the sins of our great grandmothers, with some gentle gossip about modern science and the Society for Useful Knowledge.[2] It was not always thus. The time has been when not only the dealers in political small-talk, but the whole mass of literary feeling and opinion, and no trifling portion of what is called the religious public, were disturbed and startled by the successive charges of the *Edinburgh* light-horse volunteers in their sky-blue uniforms and yellow facings.

What we have to say upon the causes of this change must be merely incidental, as the main subject of the present paper is the mental character of Mr. Jeffrey, the boldest and most bustling of these redoubted cavaliers.

Mr. Jeffrey's name first became known as that of an anonymous critic (anonymous to the world in general, from the omission of an avowed name to his articles, but sufficiently known to all the literary circles of Europe). He came into life with the kind of cleverness and the degree of self-confidence naturally produced by conflict only with men of his own age and stamp in literary and debating societies. In these he had found little to call out the higher powers of the mind, or the nobler moral capacities; among very young, and not very learned men, he can scarcely have encountered any antagonist over whom he

[1] *Athenaeum* (23 January 1828). Francis Lord Jeffrey (1773-1830), a Scottish judge who, with Sydney Smith and Henry Brougham, founded the *Edinburgh Review* (1802-1929). Jeffrey edited the famous and powerful Whig organ for twenty-seven years.

[2] The Society for the Diffusion of Useful Knowledge was largely the work of Henry Brougham.

could not triumph, at least in appearance, by his ready and ingenious volubility and the resources of a fertile, though rather
flippant, fancy. He was therefore admirably qualified to be the
editor of a new *Review*. His profusion of plausible language
would enable him to supply with ease and decency any accidental deficiency of matter; his levity in the treatment of grave
subjects would make them amusing, if not instructive, to the
meanest capacity; and the careless impudence of his editorial
colouring was excellently calculated to lend the appearance of
conscious superiority even to the blunders and inanities of his
associates.

The *Review* accordingly appeared and bore in every line the
traces of Mr. Jeffrey's superintendence. Airy ridicule or solemn
banter, the declamatory roar, the decisive dogma, the sly half-
masked inuendo — all and each were employed alternately or
together; so that the sufferings of authors, and the applause of
the public, were equally obvious and unprecedented. No single
book probably ever made so decided and general a sensation. It is
not wonderful that a knot of young men reeking from the pleas-
urable exertions of debating societies and the delight of mutual
applause, should have been led into taking that tone of decision
and defiance which is the main secret of their first success. It is
still less to be marvelled at that the shouts and gratulations of the
whole mob of literature should have urged them to still bolder
enterprises. Least of all will a wise man be surprised at the triumph of the *Edinburgh* reviewers when he considers the state of
the public mind to which they addressed themselves, and the
nature of the instruments they used.

Mr. Jeffrey appeared before the world[3] at a time when the
minds of men were all afloat; not indeed resolutely bent, as at
the period of the Reformation, upon a voyage of discovery; but
wandering at the will of the breezes and the billows, and now and
then unconsciously following for a moment the guidance of some
self-appointed pilot, or the course of some hidden current. In
politics, the overpowering interest and frightful nearness of the
French Revolution had destroyed men's belief in principles, and
absorbed their anxiety in the contemplation of mighty and terrible events. The aristocracy of this country, moreover, had felt
or thought themselves in such imminent peril that they had
exerted all their influence over the public mind; and by the aid of

[3]The *Edinburgh Review* was founded in 1802.

newspapers and debates, political dinners, and bloody battles, had succeeded in making every appearance of sympathy with the people, or attempt at speculation on the theory of government, in the highest degree unpopular and unfashionable.

The *Edinburgh Review,* accordingly, instead of opposing itself to an anti-revolutionary horror which, though just in itself, was then carried infinitely too far, assumed and held for several years a high aristocratical and monarchical tone of opinion. This was only modified by its becoming the tool and organ of a party. The political discussions of the *Edinburgh Review* have thus been always based upon the narrow system of a particular sect; and we doubt whether it has ever contained a single article tending to enlarge or exalt men's views of the social interests of their species.

In criticism, before Mr. Jeffrey became notorious for his attempts to philosophize upon poetry, this country had been fed upon such weak and mawkish spoon meat that it is no wonder that we did not for some time discover how really vague, unsubstantial, and unsatisfactory were the speculations of this celebrated author. Anyone who looks back to his writings from the vantage ground on which we now stand will readily perceive that, under a considerable appearance of freshness and novelty and of a tendency to look at poetry in connection with the nature of the human mind instead of with the rules of the critics, there is really to be found little more than an elaborate attention to details, a wish to conciliate the appearance of originality with a real determination to oppose no popular prejudice, and a want of any fine discrimination between the essential characteristics of great authors.

His disgraceful obstinacy in depreciating Wordsworth,[4] and exaggerating the merits of various men of undeniable elegance of mind but of no creative power whatsoever, is lamentable proof of wilfulness and prejudice. He has given us no tolerable estimate of the merits of any living poet, except perhaps Mr. Moore,[5] whom

---

[4] For twenty-five years, Jeffrey consistently ridiculed "the Lakers", his criticisms gradually focusing on Wordsworth. For representative depreciations, see his articles in the *Edinburgh Review:* "Thalaba, the Destroyer . . . Southey", I (October, 1802), 63-83; "Madoc, a Poem . . . Southey", VII (October, 1805), I-28; "Poems in Two Volumes. By William Wordsworth, Author of the Lyrical Ballads", XI (October, 1807), 214-231; "The Excursion . . . Wordsworth", XXIV (November, 1814), I-30.

[5] See "Lalla Rookh, an Oriental Romance", *Edinburgh Review,* XXIV (November, 1817), I-35.

his mind is exactly calculated to appreciate. In this case, the want of profoundness, both of thought and feeling in the critic becomes of less importance, from the absence of anything in the poet on which it could be exercised; while all Mr. Jeffrey's liveliness, prettiness, and neatness of mind, are brought into full play by the corresponding qualities in the object of his admiration.

But if we had time to enter into a detailed examination of the indications which Mr. Jeffrey has given of his metaphysical, moral, and religious opinions, we should have to lead our readers through a long and grave discussion of matters at present, we fear, very unlikely to suit the taste of general society. The whole structure of Mr. Jeffrey's mind is eminently French, and the only books in the higher departments of speculation for which he seems to feel a thorough liking are the works of French philosophers. It is a singular illustration of the spirit of the times that, while this is undeniably true, he should yet have been one of the most earnest champions for the strength and freedom of our older poetry.

Nevertheless, the whole tone of his writings seems to us to be redolent of his fondness for the solemn flippancy and sparkling commonplaces which abound in the works of Voltaire, Diderot, and Helvétius.[6] His philosophy is, like theirs, of the stamp which brings everything from without, and sees in the human mind nothing more precious or powerful than an empty receptacle for those dead forms which are borne in upon it by the external world. We have not at present the opportunity of following out all the conclusions as to his mind, which may be derived from this principle and which are verified in every page of his writings. But we have no doubt that it is very closely connected with the absence of all warm moral enthusiasm, the contempt for all plans of wide political amelioration, and the recourse for the elements of human virtue, not to any native strength or high aspirations within us, but to subtle calculations of consequences, whereby he would substitute for the definite and unchangeable rule, that the right is always the expedient, the maxim of the knave and the fool, or rather of that compound of both — the sophist, that the expedient is always the right.[7]

---

[6] In mid-eighteenth-century France Diderot and Helvétius published L'Encyclopédie, to which both Voltaire and Rousseau contributed. Jeffrey is clearly a "minion" of the century (see I, 2, above).

[7] Jeffrey's philosophy is one of circumstance and expediency: see VIII, 14.

The only virtues which have been much insisted upon by Mr. Jeffrey, as far as we remember, are good-nature and family affection. These are doubtless excellent things and we very sincerely believe that Mr. Jeffrey is himself a conspicuous and most amiable example of the qualities which he delights to honour in his writings. But how small a portion are they of all which is demanded from us by God, our consciences, and society; and how much may a man be distinguished for what is commonly called good-nature, and for the fulfilment of ordinary domestic duties, without ever dreaming of accomplishing a tithe of that good which is within the reach of every one. Humility, self-denial, vigorous unceasing exertion for the benefit of others — these are duties imposed upon every man.

Instead of this, the *Edinburgh Review* has exhibited to us under Mr. Jeffrey's guidance the wanton indulgence in a most criminal vanity at the expense of the reputation and feelings of authors, of all the moral delicacy of its readers, and very often of truth on the part of its writers. It scarcely contains a page which does not attempt to depress, either by contemptuous silence, grave argument, or flippant ribaldry, every emotion and principle that spreads itself beyond the narrow circuit of our external and personal interest. And almost all the men of our day who have attempted to widen the petty confines of our former intellectual and moral domain, however they may have been different in other respects, yet have been uniformly treated with the same contempt by Mr. Jeffrey. Lessing, Goethe, Coleridge, Wordsworth, Godwin[8] — there probably are scarcely any names connected in our memories with systems and peculiarities so discordant — and by what singular combination of circumstances is it that Mr. Jeffrey has united his reputation, whatever it may be, with the recollection of his abuse, or at least his contempt of these men, who are among the wisest and the greatest of our age?

To them the evil is nothing, for their glory and their usefulness are nourished in a far different atmosphere from that of declaimers and reviewers and ephemeral ribaldry. Their fame has already become a part of the empyrean galaxy, whence they shed upon

---

[8]Lessing (1729-81), a critic who emancipated German literature from the French classical school, and Goethe (1749-1832) who, as a symbol of German liberalism, influenced both Scott and Carlyle. As a treatise on liberalism, Godwin's *Enquiry Concerning Political Justice* (1793) profoundly influenced Maurice's contemporaries, while the bold inclusion of Wordsworth and Coleridge among "the wisest and greatest of our age" was a direct refutation of Jeffrey.

the dusty pathways of this workaday world a consolatory influence and holy dew. The sting and bitterness are all reserved for
the writer who has corrupted his own mind to such vile uses and
perverted to such widely mischievous ends that instrument, so
powerful for good or for evil, with which his hands were in-
trusted. The real misery is for him, and for those of his readers
who may have imbibed from him any portion of that scornful
and careless indifference to all that is most profoundly important
to man's nature; which, in almost any age but ours, would have
broadly marked out from all his contemporaries the editor of the
Edinburgh Review.

In fine, the peculiarities of Mr. Jeffrey's mind appear to us to
be extremely prominent and well defined. He has little of genial
and joyous wit, absolutely nothing of pure imagination, very
little of the power of abstraction, but a good deal of ability for
sarcasm and repartee, a graceful and glittering fancy, a singular
talent for clear distribution and lively illustration, and a very
vivid apprehension of the outward and formal differences of
minds so superior to his own that he has never been able to
conceive their earnestness, strength, and majesty. And here, in
fact, consists his essential incapacity to be an instrument of any
wide and permanent good; that he has felt within himself so
feeble and casual an action of those nobler moral and religious
propensities which are the glory and consummation of our nature, as to be utterly incapable of flinging himself boldly and
decidedly, and with an utter sacrifice of merely personal objects,
into any high and unfrequented path of exertion; and as is especially remarkable in his attempts to estimate the rarer and
mightier spirits of our age, he seems to have a mind as hard and
dead as the nether mill-stone to the impression of that highest
order of genius, which alone offers us a subject of study uniformly pregnant and inexhaustible.[9]

---

[9]When Wordsworth's *The River Duddon . . . and Other Poems* appeared, *Blackwood's
Edinburgh Magazine,* VII (May, 1820) wrote: "The age has unquestionably produced a
noble band of British Poets. . . . Scott, Byron, Wordsworth, Southey, and Coleridge.
. . . Yet, when a man asks himself, what has really been said . . . concerning any one of
these poets — how lamentably must we feel the worthlessness of all the criticism of the
most critical age ever the world produced. . . . Who can suppose for a moment that the
applauses of our Reviewers have contributed a single iota to the splendours of the
reputation of the highest? . . ." See Elsie Smith, *An Estimation of William Wordsworth
by his contemporaries 1793-1822* (1932), p. 318.

SKETCH III

Mr. Southey[1]

A poet, a biographer, a writer of literary miscellanies, an anti-quarian, a translator, an historian of campaigns, and churches, and nations, a celebrated and voluminous reviewer, himself the object of frequent and bitter criticism; in his youth the framer of ideal republics, in his manhood the advocate of desolating wars and political monopolies, in his age the chronicler of Methodism and martyrs,[2] throughout life, as a member of private society, the most uniformly amiable and pure and, at the same time, the fiercest and most unrelenting follower of a public faction: — such are the various characters in which Mr. Southey stands before the public.

To speak of such a person is a task not to be undertaken with levity; for the fame of a good man is a treasure to his race no less than to himself and ought, above all things, to be holy from the touch of the slightest misrepresentation. In this spirit we trust to write; and if, as we must, we shall offend some by too much praise of Mr. Southey, and others by too much blame; and espe-cially if we shall wound his own vanity, we can only hope that neither the public nor himself will be so uncandid as to attribute our errors to anything but a mistaken judgment, always anxious to be set right.

We have no pretensions to any private knowledge of Mr. Southey's life and really can say nothing as to the portions of his mind which do not display themselves in his works, except that we are acquainted, as is all the world, with those descriptions of his domestic wisdom and kindness which we owe to more than one of his eminent contemporaries. In other respects, we judge

[1] *Athenaeum* (29 January 1828). At the age of twenty, Robert Southey (1774-1843) began his career in a glow of liberal idealism as he and Coleridge planned their Utopian pantisocracy. By 1813 when he became Poet Laureate, he was a strong supporter of the Establishment.

[2] Maurice is referring to Southey's *Life of Wesley* (1820) and *The Book of the Church* (1824).

him from his writings alone. He brought with him into manhood, if not a peculiar robustness of intellect, yet a singular healthiness of feeling. He then had, and he happily still preserves, a strong sense of the presence and goodness of God, whose existence he seems to have found manifested, not amid the dissections of the anatomist, nor in the crucible of the chemist, nor in anything appertaining to the order of this visible world, but as a life and power in the depths of his own heart. He saw the Deity in every-thing around him because he felt his spirit eternally within him: and his sympathy with man forbade him to believe that religion was a thing of external symbols, dogmatic creeds, and endowed establishments — an excrescence on our nature appropriated to those who happen to have been educated under certain external influences and to have been born members of particular sects.

He was conscious of the germs of a higher state of being than the actual, moving and growing in his own mind; comparing these intimations of possible glory with the condition of humanity around him, he was eager to push mankind boldly forward in the path of regeneration, to pour out before the world his appeals against the tyrannies and corruptions of society and, if possible, even to realize and substantiate beneath the eyes of men the phantasm of a more harmonious and pregnant system. But the resolution to accomplish this great work at a single plunge, in-stead of labouring soberly and earnestly through life and catching at every occasion as it rose, could not support itself except by a violent and self-exhausting excitement. While, on the other hand, to maintain an unceasing and, often, an obscure and unapplauded warfare against all the myriad universal evils of our present social organization, requires more sedateness of enthusiasm than Mr. Southey seems to have possessed.[3] The ardour of his aspirations declined; and he began to look out for circumstances in the condition of things around him to which he might attach his philanthropical longings, and console himself by a notion of their excellence, for the loss of his former visions of ideal perfection.

The tendency to his former unsectarian catholicism of religion still continued in some degree to animate his mind, and has given

---

[3]In some respect, according to Jack Simmons, *Southey* (1945), p. 153, Southey "saw further than the optimistic Liberals of his day, who so obviously had the angels with them. He argued that [democracy] bred a greedy, selfish class of capitalists who, with their hangers-on, 'would care nothing for the honour and independence of England'." At the age of twenty-three, Maurice here disagrees with Southey, but he grew more cautious, and in 1854 he initiated schemes for the training of workers.

all that they have of moral value to his poetical writings. This enabled him to imbue with love, humility, and strength of heart, many of the personages whom he introduces in his longer poems, and alone lent to his tales any of that thrilling atmosphere of real existence with which his utter want of mere dramatic power would otherwise have prevented him from inspiring them. But for this feeling of brotherhood with all mankind, which teaches him to see in God an essential love breathing into all men a capacity for higher than earthly things, and not the mere founder of the Church of England, and a name to be flung in the teeth of modern atheists, — his poems would be little more than heaps of passages from old books of travels, diluted into loose and eccentric metre. But his natural piety has taught him to see in the external world much of what it really embodies of lovely and delightful, and in the heart of man an inexhaustible fountain of magnificent hopes and gentle impulses; and from these he has extracted the sweet substance of some of the most graceful and gorgeous narratives that the present generation of poets have produced. We do not, indeed, hold him to be a poet of the highest class; and his mind is fundamentally so inferior to those of Spenser and Shakespeare, Milton and Wordsworth, that we scarce remember a better illustration of the difference between first-rate and second-rate men.

The masters of ideal creation have doubtless given us in their writings either a fragment of that universe which, with all its mysteries and complications, lies so much brighter in the mind of a man of genius than before the thoughts of society, — or some mighty truth of our nature which grew up in their bosoms with all its pomp of symbol, and allusion, and shadowy story, till it swelled out and blossomed upon the world, — or some epitome of humanity such as Hamlet, or Faust, or the hero of the *Excursion,* connected with earth and daily interests by weaknesses and necessities, but gazing and struggling upward, and in whom the involved threads of hopes and doubts twist themselves with the vast web of universal being, and stretch away into its dim abysses; they have always, in short, given us a manifestation of that genius, the elements of whose power are truth and love, displaying itself through outward and accidental forms, the lifeless matter which the poet piles or scatters around him at his will, but never putting these forward as objects of interest in themselves, and unconnected with the spirit of which they are the conduit, and the laws of which they are the type. Not the stone on which the commandments were engraved lent them their importance, nor would, though it had been jasper or emerald — neither was it the lightning, nor the cloud, nor the summit of the holy mountain quaking with the revelation, but the presence of the Power which sat behind the flame and the darkness, and which stamped its wisdom on the dead tablets.

Mr. Southey seems first to have determined to write a poem, not with any high and solemn purpose, but connected with some particular age or country, which would supply him with a splendid phantasmagoria of scenery; then to have brought together from books all the descriptions and incidents that could be introduced; and lastly, to have thought of personages who, as the offspring of an elegant and amiable mind, partake of its pure and benevolent nature, but so as to appear mere abstractions of virtue, not beings of mingled character and mysterious destiny with a thousand aimless yearnings, and a thousand haughty hopes, and vague yet delightful sympathies mingled with degrading propensities and passionate selfishness. He displays a vast variety of scenic pomp; but, in general, it seems as if his personages were brought there for the sake of showing the prospect to his readers: just as in our pantomimes, the jokes, and life, and character, are omitted, and two or three mutes walk along the stage, while the scene displays to us a moving picture of seas and cities, triumphs and enchantments.

Our readers then understand that we consider Mr. Southey a poet of no higher than the second order — a judgment which we have come to when estimating him by his best and not by his worst poems, by *Roderick*[4] and *Kehama*[5], not by the *Vision of Judgment*[6], or the *Tale of Paraguay* [1825]. Yet, though we think his poetry inferior to that of many other English authors, it seems to us to display his mind in a more nearly perfect state than we find it in any of his other kinds of writing. As mere composition, the verse is far from being so faultless as the prose. But the feeling displayed in *Thalaba*[7] is incomparably better than

---

[4] *Roderick, the Last of the Goths* (1814).

[5] *The Curse of Kehama* (1810).

[6] Southey's inflated tribute to George III, *A Vision of Judgment,* evoked Byron's *The Vision of Judgment* (both poems, 1821).

[7] *Thalaba, the Destroyer* (1801).

that of the *Quarterly Review*[8], the *Book of the Church* [1824],
or the *History of the Peninsular War* [1823-32]. There is in his
poetry none of the bitterness of the daily bread earned for themselves by the followers of a faction. In it he does not write with
the perpetual consciousness that he is the gladiator of a sect or a
party: we do not see him constantly spitting gall and venom at
everyone who differs from himself in religion or politics: he feels
no yoke but the easy one of our common humanity; is moved by
no passion but the love of goodness, and gentleness, and truth;
and looks at mankind, not as followers or enemies of a particular
ecclesiastical establishment; not as republicans, or royalists, or
aristocrats, but as heirs of one nature, brethren of one house, and
partakers of one blessed hope.[9]

When we consider Mr. Southey in any other light than as a
poet, we confess that we feel a degree of sorrow in which many
of our readers will hardly sympathise. It seems to us that everything was correct in his mind at the beginning of his career,
except an excessive vanity, and a want of courage to stand before
the world but as a member of a party — but for these qualities,
we believe that a future the most honourable and useful might
well have been predicted to him. But he began to think that
political perfection was confined to our own Constitution, and
that Christianity was identical with the English Church Establishment. From that time, he has daily become more and more of a
partisan — daily more and more of a sectarian. It is easy to say
that he admires the present form of the British government because he thinks it the best calculated to produce national happiness; and that he lauds endowments and pluralities because he
believes them most consonant to the apostolical model; but it is
evident from the whole tone of his writings that the actual objects of his respect and love are not good government and true
Christianity for themselves, but good government and true religion as by law established — in short, Church and State — the
aristocracy and the bench of bishops.

Thence the habit of the politician of abusing everyone, however sincerely attached to the interests of mankind, who has
attempted to reform the government of his own country, or

[8] From 1808, Southey contributed regularly to this Tory Review.

[9] Here, in embryo, is Maurice's Christian social philosophy. Always opposed to parties
and sects he, like Coleridge and the *poetic* Southey, saw human beings as "heirs of
one nature".

thinks that we ought to attempt it in ours. Thence the fondness of the theologian for swelling the bodies of his sentences with "the Church of England" while he puts Providence into a parenthesis. And thence above all, the violence, we had almost said the malignity otherwise so utterly inexplicable, displayed by a pious and benevolent man against all from whom he differs, of every period and denomination: against, that is, nine-tenths of all sects and parties and especially against those wiser and better men who, seeing in the spirit of sectarianism one of the greatest afflictions of humanity, have sedulously avoided its enslaving and corrupting influence.

He is indeed a mournful example of the ruin which may be wrought upon the fairest minds by attaching an universal feeling to particular institutions, and by professing to find all truth in the creed of one establishment. In this case the whole spiritual nature of man is narrowed into an almost mechanical clinging to a few valueless sounds, the images perhaps of nothing either in earth or heaven but of the stupid bigotry that invented them. The attributes of Deity become the watchwords of intolerance and uncharitableness — and Christianity itself, instead of being a scheme for the perfecting of our nature into purity and love, is changed into a volume of dissonant war-cries, while "the whole armour of God" is employed for the unhallowed strife of worldly passions.

It is obvious also that, in politics, so soon as ceasing to look forward for improvement and the activity of Mr. Southey's mind attached itself to things as they are, he began to look back into the past, to find supports for his opinion: and because he wished to make out that the present government is a good one, he perverts the whole aspect of history. Strafford and Laud were put to death by political reformers; and therefore, out of hatred to all reform and as a means of bringing dislike on modern innovators, Strafford becomes a martyr to his benevolent and unselfish patriotism; and the sickening blood-thirstiness of Laud is to be buried in eternal oblivion.[10] We doubt not that Mr. Southey is quite sincere in thinking that a purely aristocratic constitution is the best possible form of government. But moved by this conviction,

[10]Thomas Wentworth (1593-1641), first Earl of Strafford and court favourite, and William Laud (1573-1645), Archbishop of Canterbury, were both in the service of Charles I and, like the king, they were beheaded by the Long Parliament in its determination to end the personal government of the monarch. Southey, a Tory, sympathizes with the royalists, whereas Maurice, promoting reform, spurns Southey's attitude.

he speaks of all who think otherwise with an abhorrence which
he probably justifies to himself by the consideration that they
are enemies to the happiness of mankind, without reflecting that
other men may honestly think just as ill of his opinions as he of
theirs, and that neither party would be excusable in slandering
and misrepresenting the other.

In spite of the excesses into which Mr. Southey has been betrayed, his natural kindness breaks out very frequently through
the fretful load of prejudices and dislikes wherewith years of
partisanship have encumbered him: while his propensity to vitu-
peration usually displays itself most strongly on the points with
regard to which he has himself been in the habit of disputing. He
hates Roman Catholics, he hates Calvinists, he hates Unitarians,
he hates Frenchmen who, in his eyes, are almost all atheists and
Jacobins; he thinks the Whigs a very dangerous set of men, he
believes that the *Edinburgh Review* is possessed by Satan, and
above all, he abhors everyone who dreams of introducing any
reforms into England.

Yet with all this, we verily believe few men would take more
trouble to confer a service on the people of Mexico, or Arabia, or
even, if an opportunity presented itself, would seize with more
anxiety an opportunity of doing good to his enemies. The *Edinburgh Review* has uniformly dealt him hard and unjust measure;[11] and all his political opponents have been eager enough to
return the blows which he has shown the example of inflicting;
and though his attacks on Lord Byron are very silly, his Lordship
disgraced himself and disgusted the better portion of his readers
by the brutality with which *he* carried on the war.[12] It is not
very wonderful therefore that a person who, however amiable
and by no means remarkable for humility, should have frequently lost temper against these antagonists. But what we complain of
is that on all occasions when he happens to have an occasion for
wounding the feelings of those who are at least towards him
guiltless, he displays precisely the same malevolence, and that no
man can expect to be treated with ordinary candour who does
not agree with him on every possible subject, repeat the Laureate
creed,[13] and bow before the Keswick idols.[14]

[11] See II, 4 above.

[12] Simmons, *Southey,* pp. 141, 167-71.

[13] Southey's beliefs.

[14] Southey and Coleridge, who had married sisters, lived at Greta Hall, Keswick. The
idols are the prejudices that Southey "worships".

Whatever be his faults he must, as long as he lives and writes, continue to be a popular author. As a mere controversialist (the most melancholy mockery of humanity we know, except the monkeys of Exeter 'Change[15]) his abilities and information can never be despised; though in this department (the garrets) of literature, he shows to the least advantage. He has abundant information, and a ready grace in applying it; but he wants the subtlety of argumentation and bitterness of sarcasm, which are so large ingredients in the finished polemic. He generally substitutes for reasoning mere assertion and authority, and downright abuse for satire.

The construction of his sentences, the clearness of his arrangement, and the liveliness of his narrative are admirably adapted for history. But from the want of all power of philosophising, he looks at events as naked facts rather than as developments of principles; or if he ever recurs to general laws, they are of the most commonplace description. As a writer of biographies and of essays of amusing information scarcely anyone, we believe, ever excelled him. His *Life of Nelson* [1813] has been much praised, but not more than it deserves, for unaffected simplicity and unexaggerated earnestness.

His writings probably cover more paper than those of anyone now living, except indeed the gentleman in the farce, who "has written all the newspapers in Europe for many years." They contain a wonderful mass of elegant composition and pleasant research, of lively description and animated narrative; but when we consider the effect they must have had in rendering popular his narrow system of politics and religion, we are reluctantly compelled to doubt whether they have not, on the whole, accomplished more of evil than of good.

He has long announced a book on a more fruitful and difficult subject than any that he has previously treated of, *The Progress and Prospects of Society;*[16] but though we shall be curious to see

[15] Exeter 'Change in the Strand, London, a building complex with "two walks below stairs, and as many above, with shops on each side". The last tenant of the "upper rooms" kept a menagerie, and here, in March 1826, Chunee, the famous elephant was shot. Maurice may be referring not to the monkeys in the menagerie, but to the men who, in putting down the elephant, behaved with sub-human intelligence, thus making a "melancholy mockery of humanity". See Henry B. Wheatley, *London Past and Present* (1891), ii, 25 and, for the account of Chunee's death, William Hone, *The Every-Day Book* (1827), ii, 322-336.

[16] *Sir Thomas Moore: or Colloquies on the Progress and Prospects of Society* appeared in 1829.

him make the experiment, we would advise him, as he values his reputation, to think well before he publishes such a work. It is all very well to talk of the balance of the Constitution and the arm of Providence revealing itself in our favour in the Peninsular war[17] when, as in the *Quarterly Review,* there are facilities[18] for assuming conclusions and escaping from proofs; but it will not do in a separate and formal discussion of the powers and destiny of the human race, a subject which has employed the greatest men the world has ever known from Plato until our own day. On such a subject it will not be sufficient to represent irresponsible aristocracies as the saints that shall inherit the earth, or to clothe the angels of the world in lawn-sleeves and a cassock.

On the whole, Mr. Southey's chief talent appears to us to be style. Though sometimes a little affected, and even that but rarely, his composition on the whole is wonderfully clear, careful, and animated. But here, we are afraid, the chief part of our praise stops — for he has no wit and very little eloquence — qualities, by the by, which generally go together. He has none of the sprightly fancy of Mr. Moore — none of the elevating imagination of Wordsworth. He never could have written half as much as he has if his books required any great expense of thought; but they really appear to us to exhibit none at all; and the research they display, though laborious and astonishingly extensive, yet costs infinitely less of real intellectual toil and weariness than the deducing subtle conclusions from vast and complicated premises, and the binding together and arranging masses of disjointed facts by the application of great general laws. But Mr. Southey, happily for his present ease, fame, and profit, has no such troublesome propensity.

He seems, in fact, to have a fainter conception of anything like abstract speculation than any living author of nearly equal celebrity, except only his sole competitor in quantity of writing — Sir Walter Scott. And it must necessarily be so. Great thinkers express wide principles in few words. But nine-tenths of all the events and personages chronicled by the poet-laureate do not appear in his pages such as naturally connect themselves with any universal principle or permanent consciousness of the human mind, and do not seem to have been the occasion of any feeling

[17]Britain under Arthur Wellesley (later, the Duke of Wellington) drove Napoleon from Spain, 1808-14.

[18]Anonymity and levity, for example.

in his breast but contempt for some rival dogmatist, or exultation over some inaccurate historian.

Few of his works can live among future generations. For the subjects of his writings, the selfish wars of governments, and the religious systems that narrow themselves into creeds, except as warnings to be shuddered at, must happily lose their interest for our children.[19] But we confess we regret that his poetry is not of a more condensed and concentrated character; for there is a delicacy and sweetness of feeling and a splendour of descriptive diction which, if less diluted and impoverished by verbiage so as to outlast the fluctuations of the hour, would give as much delight to all future ages as they have already conferred on the instructed and gentle of our own day.

[19] A correct prognosis, made in the teeth of Southey's high reputation in 1828.

SKETCH IV

Mr. Cobbett[1]

There never has been an European nation in which this writer could have arisen and have been what he is, for so long a time, except only the dominions of George IV.[2] He has existed by nothing but the freedom of the press; and therefore England alone, or revolutionary France, could have furnished him with the necessary field. In France his talents would have placed him at the head of a party, and he would have found the shoulders of his supporters but steps to the guillotine. But it is in England, and here only, that he could have been produced — here only that he could become what he is, the ablest of mob writers, the least successful of public men; the opponent whose abuse is the most virulent, and at the same time the least regarded; the most vigorous adversary of the aristocracy, yet the most despised laughing-stock of the people; the most uniformly obnoxious to the general mind, yet the most strenuous friend to every time-honoured prejudice; the politician who with the largest fertility of talent and the most unwearied industry has failed in everything he has undertaken; and yet with a kind of blundering omnipotence, still continues to amuse, to excite, and sometimes even to terrify society. Without a great mass of democratic opinion he would have had nothing on which to act or whereby to sustain himself; without considerable freedom of discussion he never could have wielded his weapons; but for the general consciousness of great evils in our social system, he would have wanted objects which men could endure to hear denounced; and if we were not governed by the deeply founded predominance of an

---

[1] *Athenaeum* (12 February 1828). William Cobbett (1763-1835), a self-educated labourer, was an effective though unofficial leader of the working-class agitation for reform until he ultimately became M. P. for Oldham. See G. M. Trevelyan, "Cobbett's England (1793-1832)", *English Social History* (1944), chapters XV and XVI, and G. D. H. Cole, *The Life of William Cobbett* (1947).

[2] George IV (1820-1830): the decade of the king's reign is the period of Maurice's concern in *Sketches*.

aristocracy, his abilities must at some time or other have enabled him to profit by occasion, and perhaps to raise a permanent power on a popularity which has now long departed, and for ever.

Mr. Cobbett is the natural out-growth of our soil; and as he could not have existed in any other country, so he can scarcely be understood by any but Englishmen. In France, Italy, and Spain, the body who misgovern the nation have little power of perverting the opinions of the instructed classes, and therefore politics in these countries have been commonly studied as a science, and reduced to general principles. These are taken for granted by the persons who would now discuss such subjects, and the attempt to argue on any other grounds would only produce contempt and ridicule. But as the class by whom political power is held in this country are an aristocracy,[3] supported partly by wealth, the combined influence of these enables them to guide in a great degree the direction of public opinion, and prevent the universal reception of any determinate political maxims to which everyone might at once appeal in any question of the abuse of authority. This accounts in a great degree for the extreme ignorance and vacillation of Mr. Cobbett's reasonings, and also for the favourable reception which some of them have met with.

But the indifference to wide and abstract truth with regard to men's social interests is by no means the only cause for the occasional popularity and constant notoriety of this singular author. He is really a man of very rare and particularly applicable abilities. He knows nothing, to be sure, of metaphysics, and is not very deeply versed in the higher mathematics. We doubt whether he could write a Greek ode, or price a Raphael, or comprehend Faust. But on ordinary political subjects his argument is wonderfully lucid and powerful. He deduces his conclusions so shortly that we never lose sight of their connection with the premises. He states his reasoning in such homely and energetic language, and so impregnates it with all the force of the feeling which he wished to excite, sets it in such a variety of lights, strengthens it with so much of fresh familiar illustration, and sharpens it with such cutting sarcasm, that there probably never was a writer whose paragraphs, taken singly, are so well calculated to carry along the minds of the less instructed classes: and besides the qualities we have mentioned there is, through all

[3] Whose power was to be curtailed by the Reform Bill of 1832.

his works, an easy and negligent superiority which gives an imposing look of conscious power.

The most characteristic of his distinctions undoubtedly is that he never wrote a sentence which is not intelligible at the first glance. The next point which marks him out from all the other authors of the time is the inimitable energy of his scurrility: a merit the display of which is certainly not restrained by any very scrupulous delicacy, but shows itself in so bold-faced an exuberance that, if one were inclined to make a dictionary of our language, divided into different classes of words, the commercial, the metaphysical, the laudatory, and so forth, a complete catalogue of the vituperative might certainly be collected from the writings of Mr. Cobbett. His third great glory is an unparalleled impudence, an effrontery so excessive as absolutely to have in it something of the awful. It is not the peasant trampling upon princes, nor the corporal treating the Duke of Wellington with an easy superiority; but the man of a thousand inconsistencies and an almost universal ignorance, quietly taking for granted as a matter settled years ago that he himself, and he alone, is the fountain of all wisdom, that he holds in his hands the fate of England, and that he has prophesied, to the letter, everything which was, and is still to happen upon earth. This it is which sets our author at such an immeasurable distance above everyone else, that he is undoubtedly the most amusing of mountebanks — the most sublime of quacks.

The great defect of his mind (barring common honesty) is his utter incapacity to generalize. He has a peculiar hatred to broad principles — partly because they require the exertion of a larger intellect than his — partly because if he ever recognized one such rule, he might find it an inconvenient restraint on his future laxity of lucubration; but chiefly, we believe, because he came upon the political stage with the formed habits of early life which taught him to apply to every particular case, for itself, a sort of overbearing clownish shrewdness such as is nourished among fields and farm-yards, speaks the language of the country market, and savours of crops and cattle. He never, therefore, attempts to compress into his robust and homespun sentences any guiding or standard propositions; but with the most ostentatiously simple subtlety, narrows to the uttermost the premises, or widens the conclusion, and by some bold knock-down reference to partial experience connects the one or the other with the cause or the consequence he aims at. It is thus that the whole

existing universe, God and Mammon, ploughmen and placemon-
gers, the debts and the bishops, figure alternately in every page as
the origin and result of themselves and one another: while
William Cobbett, of Long Island, Botley, or Kensington,[4] stands
superior (like an oracular oak) amid this rigmarole pageantry of
all created things, and announces that, if the people will but buy
his pamphlets, and the King make him Prime Minister, he will
finally overmaster the principle of evil, drive paper-money from
the world, and re-establish the age of gold.

Therefore, when anything he wishes to prove is contrary to a
commonly received political law, instead of attempting to show
how and why this is erroneous, he thinks it sufficient to say that
it is put forth by "Scotch *feelosofers*",[5] or that it is "the spawn
of the beastly borough-mongering faction" and, therefore, utterly unworthy of his consideration. It is chiefly to this want that
we must attribute the ephemeral nature of his influence, and the
neglect which consigns Mr. Cobbett's speculations about passing
events to the oblivion of the last week's playbill and the last
year's almanac.

He is also entirely deficient in imagination.[6] It is a faculty that
can only exist as the organ and interpreter of deep feelings and
much-embracing thoughts: it is denied to ribald levity and systematic dogmatism: it is like the allegories of ancient mythology,
or the temple of the Lord at Jerusalem, a rich treasure-house of
symbols for things infinite and invisible: it is, as was sinless
Paradise, a garden built of the bright relics of former beauty, and
fruitful of the types of yet unexistent perfection. It is like the
Titan[7] of old story, who framed the goodly and unblemished
body that was destined to be filled with the informing breath of
the Divine Being: for glorious as are its creations, they are mo-
tionless and lifeless except when animated by the inspiration of
truth.

[4]Cobbett lived (1792-1800) in Long Island, New York, before settling in England at
Botley, a village near Southampton, and Kensington, London.

[5]Cobbett's derogatory term for the editors of the *Edinburgh Review,* "those eulogists
and understrappers of the Whig-Oligarchy". See his *Rural Rides,* edited by Eric Fitch
Daglish (1932), p. 22: Wednesday, November 14, [1821].

[6]Maurice waxes metaphorical in describing the imagination. Aware of its redemptive
power, he is opposed to "systematic dogmatism".

[7]The Titan was a child of Uranus and Ge, Heaven and Earth — a concept felicitously
applied to the imagination. The reconciliation of opposites as the only means to truth
was a basic tenet of Maurice's creed.

But in the author whom we are now considering, as there are none of these expansive and pregnant convictions, none of these consciousnesses of the master laws of the universe; so is there none of that power whereby they might be embodied and made palpable, and which fixes its images among mankind to be not only as spots in the desert of the brightest green and most grateful shadow, but as gushing forth the waters whereat the weary and desolate may drink in health, and strength, and comfort. He scarcely ever takes us away from those wretched and trivial tumults of the hour, in which our feelings come in contact with nothing but the follies and selfishness, the outward accidents and unhappy frivolities of our kind. He is of the earth, earthy, and would chain his readers to the clod of which his own soul is a portion. He never flings into the air those spells which would display to us the multitudinous shadows that people the waste infinite, genii and ministers to the laws of external and moral nature. Almost all his writings have, therefore, a tendency to narrow and embitter our minds; and to make the weary and bleeding world tread on and on to all eternity the same thorny round of faction.

His treatment of the *History of the Protestant Reformation* [1824] is a lamentable instance of those evil propensities to which we have alluded. The men who maintain that all was wrong before the Reformation and that in Protestant countries all has been right since — who assert, or go near to assert, that the great object was then accomplished and secured; that the mystical *projection* then took place; and that the world at that time received the stamp of those lineaments which it must always wear until they are destroyed by the final conflagration — make as mere an idol of the handiwork of Huss, Wickliffe, and Luther,[8] as they charge upon the Roman Catholic that he finds in the Popedom; or as the Mohammedan erects for himself in his idea of the Prophet's mission. They would prevent us from struggling on to further improvement; and because we have set out upon the journey, would keep us tied to the first mile-stone.

The world needs much more of reformation than it has as yet received, and will ever stand in want of reformers while it contains a vestige of ignorance and sin. But the writer who denies the value of that great impulse; who says that we ought not to

___

[8]John Huss (c.1369-1415), John Wickliffe (c.1320-84), and Martin Luther (1483-1546) were religious reformers in Bohemia, England, and Germany, respectively.

keep up the progress which it aided, but to go back to the point at which it found us; who maintains that mankind are in a less hopeful condition now — when thousands of eager and searching minds are feeling round them on every side to seize the hem of the garment of Truth — than when no man was permitted to do anything but kiss the robes of the priesthood; when the world is evidently wrestling with the throes of a mighty pregnancy; — than when, in tumult and passion it conceived three centuries ago the long-borne burthen of promise — the man who, without being misled by sectarian prepossession and with an obvious party purpose, can at this day profess this doctrine, is to be classed, not with the lovers of wisdom or with the reformers of their kind, but with the noisy hounds of faction.

It is not in this way that the cause of Roman Catholic equalization ought to be conducted. It is not by turning back our eyes to the bigotries of the past that we are to learn charity for the future; it is not by imitating the barbarian tribes which deified their ancestors that we are to nourish into the image of God the generations of our descendants; it is not, in short, by vindicating the sectarianism of a sect, be it Roman Catholic, Protestant, or Hindu, that we must teach ourselves universal toleration; but by looking at all men, not as members of sects, but as partakers of a common humanity, whom it will be better for us, than even for them, to bind to ourselves by the cords of love.[9]

We have dwelt upon this matter the more especially because it stands out from the other subjects of Mr. Cobbett's speculations, the occasion of a whole work[10] — a separate and marvellous instance of the narrowness of his intellect, or of that from which almost all narrowness of intellect proceeds, the viciousness of his feelings. On many other points he is equally wrong-headed. He laughs at the political economists, while it is obvious that, when writers give you the whole process of their thoughts, you ought only either to show errors in the reasoning or object to the premises. We should be inclined perhaps to quarrel with some of the primary assumptions of the economists; but these are allowed by Mr. Cobbett and built upon by himself in many of his arguments; and he scarcely ever attempts to expose any sophism or

---

[9] The Catholic Emancipation Act was passed in 1829. This paragraph, breathing "universal toleration" and "common humanity" is ecumenical in tone, and urges unity, an insistent theme in Maurice's writings.

[10] Cobbett's *Protestant Reformation,* mentioned above.

mistake in the course of their deductions

We might mention, if we had space, a variety of other matters whereupon this author is no less in error. But in fact Mr. Cobbett has at different times bestowed such exceeding pains in the attempt to refute or contradict everything he has ever maintained, that to bring his opinions into discussion here would be merely to inspire the slaughtered monsters with a galvanic life for the purpose of again meeting them in combat. Since the time when it was said by the patriarch of critics, "Oh! that mine enemy would write a book",[11] we do not believe that anyone ever has written a book containing so grotesque an array of inconsistencies as *The Political Register* [1802-35]. To compare one of its earlier, with one of its later volumes, remembering that both are written by the same hand, reminds us of those fantastic dreams wherein we fight and conquer some vague shape, which anon starts up again and engages with a shadow that wears its own former likeness.[12]

There is one great merit in Mr. Cobbett — and one only — which is perhaps peculiar to him among the party-writers of the day. There is not a page of his that ever has come under our notice, wherein there does not breathe throughout, amid all his absurdities of violence and inconsistency, the strongest feeling for the welfare of the people. The feeling is in nine cases in ten totally misdirected; but there it is, a living and vigorous sympathy with the interests and hopes of the mass of mankind.[13]

Many persons will be ready to maintain, because he has shown himself at various times as not very scrupulous for truth, that he has no real and sincere good quality whatsoever and that he merely writes what is calculated to be popular. But we confess we are inclined to think from the tone and spirit of his works that he commonly persuades himself he believes what he is saying and feels deeply at the moment what he expresses strongly. It is obvious to us that, while he puts forth against his opponents the most unmeasured malignity, there is a true and hearty kindliness in all that he writes about, or to, the people. He seems to us to

[11] Job, XXXI, 35: "Behold my desire is, that the Almighty would answer me, and that mine adversary had written a book."

[12] Cobbett began as a Tory but became a focus for reforming opinion, thus moving politically in a direction the reverse of Southey's.

[13] Cobbett always unites the head with the heart in his genuine feeling for the poor. *Cobbett's Poor Man's Friend* (1826-7) contrasts the supposed prosperity of labourers prior to the Reformation with their condition in 1826.

speak of the poorer classes as if he still felt about him the atmosphere of the cottage — not as if he were robed in ermine or lawn,
or in the sable gown of a professor — but in the smock-frock of
the peasant.

And it would be useful, therefore, to peers and bishops, parlia-
mentary orators and university dogmatists, if they would now
and then read the books they always rail at. They would find in
them a portrait, thrilling with all the pulses of animation, of the
thoughts and desires of a class, the largest and therefore the most
important in society, among whom that which is universal and
eternal in our nature displays itself under a totally different aspect from that which it wears among us. Mr. Cobbett's personal
consciousness of all which is concealed from our eyes by grey
jackets and clouted shoes, has kept alive his sympathy with the
majority of mankind; and this is indeed a merit, which can be
attributed to but few political writers.[14] And far more than this,
it is a merit which belongs to no one we remember but himself
and Burns,[15] among all the persons that have raised themselves
from the lowest condition of life into eminence.

Take, for an instance, the late Mr. Gifford,[16] and see with
what persevering dislike he opposed the interests and hopes of
the portion of society to which he himself originally belonged.
He seems to have felt the necessity of vindicating his new position by contempt for his former associates; to have proved the
sincerity of his apostacy from plebeianism by tenfold hostility to
all but the aristocracy; and to have made use of his elevation only
to trample upon those with whom he was formerly on a level.
Now we do not think that Mr. Cobbett has taken the right way
to advance the well-being of the people; but we certainly do
believe, and we think, but for prepossession everybody would
incline to think from the character of his writings, that he does
really and earnestly desire to promote the happiness of the labouring classes.

This is the bright side of his moral disposition. The one saving
elegance of his tastes is a hearty relish and admiration of outward

[14]Wordsworth made "grey jackets and clouted shoes" his primary concern in *Lyrical Ballads.*

[15]Robert Burns (1759-96).

[16]William Gifford (1756-1826), a cobbler's apprentice who rose in 1809 to become
the first editor of the *Quarterly Review,* disliked reformers and wrote embittered
criticisms of rising authors.

natural beauty. There are many portions of his voluminous works in which we seem to see the tufted greenness and fresh sparkle of the country through a more lucid medium than in any of the writings of our best novelists or travellers. This arises from the happy fact that his way of looking at things external has never been systematized.

He retains all the old glad vividness of his apprehensions, wherewith he used to look upon the fields and hedge-rows when he was a whistling plough-boy; and he puts the clouds, cows, and meadows into his pages, with the simple clearness of description that naturally results from this feeling. Men, who were more early instructed, see everything in connection with wide and vague trains of association, which dilute and confuse the direct strength of their perception. But

> The cowslip on the river's brim
> A yellow cowslip is to him,
> And it is nothing more.[17]

It is nothing more to him in the way that it is anything more to us. It is to him a little flower, which recalls no poetical descriptions, and does not suggest the images of the nymphs, or Pan, or even of elfin dancers. But it appears to him with all the firmness and liveliness of impression which it gave to his boyish senses, and so he offers it to us; and, in truth, he does his spiriting gently. But we are far off from the turbulent politician. We had wandered with him into the rich corn-field, surging and gleaming to the wind, and dappled with the shadows of the clouds — we were resting from the din of factions among the happy plenteousness and varied forms of animal enjoyment which crown the farm-yard — but the cock crows and, like uneasy ghosts, we must away.

We believe we have treated Mr. Cobbett more lightly than he would have been handled by most men. But we do not think that his gross and manifold sins are such as seem likely to be particularly mischievous at present. When the people are better educated, they will be little at the mercy of the abusive violence and ludicrous inconsistencies of such writers; or rather if, as a nation, we had been better brought up — if the Legislature and the

---

[17]A variant of Wordsworth's *Peter Bell* (11. 248-50). *Cowslip* is the common name of the *Primula veris*, the primrose. Maurice is either quoting from memory or deliberately emphasizing Cobbett's common touch.

Church Establishment had done their duty — a person with Mr. Cobbett's abilities, and in his original position, would not have grown up what he is. Had he been taught the easy wisdom of love, instead of the bitter lessons of hatred and ambition, he might, he must, have been an instrument of the most extensive and permanent good. He would have brought us nearer to the poor and lowly; he would have domesticated truth and religion at the fire-side of the cottager; he would have bound us all more closely in the embrace of common sympathy and mutual improvement.

As it is, he is merely a writer of extraordinary powers; a politician of vulgar and petty objects. There is a downright and direct simplicity in his sentences, and a copiousness of unelaborate illustration, which would render him the most perfect of writers for the people at large, if there were not in his opinions a confounding together of all systems which are not philosophical and at the bottom of his mind an indifference to truth, which have prevented him from ever doing a tithe of the good he might otherwise have accomplished. For what are his improvements in the manufacture of bonnets, his delightful *Cottage Economy* [1821-22] and his singular and powerful volume of sermons,[18] when weighed against all the misapplied influence and wasted talents, which he has been burying through life under heaps of scurrility and inconsistency? It is painful to think of all that such a man would have been induced to do under a better social system, and to compare it with the little he has effected towards regenerating a bad one.

He will doubtless say of the *Athenaeum,* if he mentions our observations at all, that "another of the brethren of the broadsheet, I suppose, some starving Scotch *feelosofer,* who has come to London to pick our pockets and help to support the THING,[19] has been writing a parcel of trash about me. A pitiful rascal, who probably never saw me in his life, unless I may have given him a penny for sweeping a crossing, and pushing his greasy hat under my nose, has pretended to give the world an account of my character. He ought to be much obliged to me for mentioning his beastly slanders, as the world would otherwise never have heard of them. As it is, he need not imagine that I shall

[18] In March 1821 appeared the first of *Cobbett's Monthly Religious Tracts,* collected in 1822 as *Cobbett's Sermons.*

[19] Government finance, which lay at the root of wide-spread social and political ills.

attempt to answer him. Though I suppose, indeed, the poor devil's only hope lay in his expectation that I never should hear of his dirty work. But my readers need not suspect that I shall condescend to notice his laughable accusations.

"All the world, except his Majesty's Ministers, have long ago acknowledged that no man but William Cobbett can save this country from utter ruin. And his Majesty's Government will soon be obliged to come sneaking to my house at Kensington, to persuade me to tell them how they can get us out of the mess. But the King knows already that I will not assist him to save England from destruction as long as he refuses to give me uncontrolled power over the THING, by making me Prime Minister. My readers know how my predictions have been accomplished; and I now prophesy that this will happen before Easter; we shall then have the *feelosofers* eating their words (and a dirty dish they make) and, till then, I leave them to the cheesemongers."

Our readers see that we write with our eyes open to the consequences of our temerity.

SKETCH V

Mr. Wordsworth[1]

With what different feelings do we write this name, from those with which it will be seen by (we fear) a large proportion of our readers! A few have read the works of Wordsworth and disapprove; many have not read them and therefore condemn; the rest, among whom are we, think of him as of one greater and purer from vulgar meannesses than to belong exclusively to our generation, and yet connected with it by deep sympathies, by a thousand gentle and strong associations, and by the noblest moral influence. Wherefore this variety of conviction? Partly because the public taste has been in a large degree formed by very different models from that presented by this great poet; partly because it has been much misled by evil guidance;[2] but chiefly because his poems require in their readers a far more majestic state of feeling, and more active exercise of reason, than are to be found among ordinary men. Of our own belief we shall now offer some explanation.

At the period of the change of dynasty in 1688, however necessary it may have been to take strong measures for the purpose of saving our bishops from martyrdom and our venerable ancestors from a popish explosion, there was at least as much need of a revolution in poetry as in government. Indeed, from the time of the death of Milton until our own generation there was scarcely a mind in England, and not one of the highest order whereof a trace remains, that dreamed of acting upon the feelings

---

[1] *Athenaeum* (19 February 1828). This sketch of William Wordsworth (1770-1850) forms the key-stone in the arch of Maurice's series. As Coleridge was so memorably impressed by the genius of Wordsworth as to be convinced "that fancy and imagination were two distinct and widely different faculties," so Maurice, applying this distinction to each of his authors, finds Wordsworth a poet of the highest order because he acts "upon the feelings through the imagination." See S. T. Coleridge, *Biographia Literaria*, edited by J. Shawcross (1965), i, 60.

[2] Of unperceptive reviewers, like Jeffrey whose attack on the *Excursion, Edinburgh Review*, XXIV (November, 1814), 1-30, roused Coleridge to write the *Biographia Literaria*. See below, V, 10.

through the imagination, by the aid of any more powerful engines than the passions and modes of reasoning which display
themselves on the surface of human intercourse and, as they
spring from nothing essential in man's nature, are perpetually
shifting and passing away.[3] The muse was dressed like a lady on a
birth-night with a toupee and patches, a stomacher and a hoop-
petticoat. Her offspring were mere vague shadows, with a certain
conventional inanity of feature; and the heroes of poetry were
only more interesting than the mutes who clear the stage between the acts of a play by being more sillily irritable, more
ludicrously fierce, and fonder of words of six syllables than are
real and living men. While the way to bring a description or event
home to the feelings of every reader, and to impress it vividly on
his imagination, was by comparing it to something in the scandalous chronicle of Greek or Roman mythology; by arraying it in a
patched garment of classical allusion; by calling a breeze "a
zephyr", and a rivulet "the Naiad of the crystal flood".[4]

The dynasty of this gentle dullness was destined, however, to
be shaken and overthrown in the midst of its most triumphant
imbecility. Three-fourths of the eighteenth century passed away
without producing in Europe a single really important political
event, or one great predominating mind. But these things were all
destined to be changed in the changes of the great moral cycle,
acting apparently through the proximate causes of various political convulsions.

The obstinate tyranny of England forced the colonies in North
America into a most just and holy rebellion.[5] A contest of principles arose; it was imitated in Ireland in the conflict which tri-
umphed in the year 1782;[6] and reproduced under a more formid-
able and astounding shape in the French Revolution.[7] Wars
became struggles of the intellects and passions of nations — not
merely of muskets and bills of exchange. Politics were changed
into the opposition of great moral principles, instead of the frivolous frenzies of pamphleteers and secretaries of state, for the

[3] Between Milton and Wordsworth, English poetry was fanciful rather than imaginative,
artificial rather than creative.

[4] Characteristic Neo-classical phraseology.

[5] The Declaration of Independence: 4 July 1776.

[6] The date of Ireland's legislative independence.

[7] The fall of the Bastille on 14 July 1789 marked the start of the French Revolution.

possession of a village or the inviolability of a sinecure. Men learned, in short, to think and to feel for themselves instead of being talking or acting mechanisms.[8]

The breath of universal existence seemed to become a subtle and mighty power, an impulse, and an inspiration. The hearts of men were enlarged by the reception of a vast hope; and their faculties impregnated by the glorious influence of the time. The great visible changes were the awakening of nations, the overthrow of the mighty, the destruction of armies and empires, the reform of France into a republic, and of Italy into a people. But there were also the stranger, more fruitful, and more permanent changes, the regeneration of the German mind, and the second miraculous descent upon English literature of the purifying and kindling fire from heaven.

Of this imbreathed spirit, Wordsworth has in our country received more largely than anyone now living; or rather bringing with him into manhood rarer faculties than the rest of his generation, he has also laboured more unceasingly and earnestly to make them instruments of ideal art and moral truth, creators of the beautiful, and ministers to the good. For these objects he has ceased to draw from the shallow and muddy fountains of so much preceding and contemporary literature. He has sequestered himself from the customary interests and busy competitions of the society around him; and has endeavoured to see, in his own breast and in the less artificial classes of mankind, the being of his species as it is, and as it might be, and in the outward world a treasury of symbols in which we may find reflections of ourselves, and intimations of the purport of all existence. He has attempted to build up in this way his own nature; and to impress it upon his kind by embodying his serene benevolence and universal sympathies in the forms supplied by a peculiarly faithful and fertile imagination.

He has not aimed at all at momentary applause, nor even made renown, either present or to be, the object of his exertions; but he has written from the love of man, the reverence for truth, and the devotion to art which, though totally unconnected with the business of book-making, are the only foundations of literary excellence. Therefore it is that, amid all the ridicule with which he who belongs not to the age has been attacked by its minions,

---

[8] Romantic concepts of freedom and organic growth supplanted those of classical formalism. The ideas of Coleridge supplemented and began to enlarge those of Hobbes and Newton.

his influence has been gradually but uniformly extending; and
those who judge everything by the commercial standard of the
day, will be surprised to find that the booksellers have lately
thought it for their advantage to publish a complete and beautiful edition of the works[9] of this "drivelling ballad-monger".[10]

The main strength of the clamour against Wordsworth has
been directed upon his fondness for the use of plain and ordinary
phraseology. Now for this there are various reasons. In the first
place, the constant employment by metrical writers of certain set
forms of phrase, many of them never used by anyone to express
real feelings, and the rest by the very fact of becoming the cant
language of poetry, disused among living men — this custom had
by repetition so deadened their effect that they had ceased to be
symbols recalling anything whatsoever but the precedents for
their use in some other writer. Wordsworth attempted to remedy
this by seeking for fresh reservoirs of expression in the real language of mankind, as springing from their genuine feelings: and
he found his best materials among those classes whom the habits
of society have not compelled to dilute into weakness the mode
of communicating their sensations; though in drawing his language in a great degree from the less instructed ranks, he of
course omitted everything that by its rarity would have been
unintelligible, or which was not in conformity either with human
nature in general or with the necessary principles of human discourse.

But it is a mistake to suppose that he never employs a dialect
which might not have been collected from the lips of ploughmen;
on the contrary, using simple phrases for simple things, and giving unpedantic expressions to uninstructed men; he also wields,
and far more powerfully than anyone between Milton and him-

---

[9] *The Poetical Works of William Wordsworth* (5 vols., London: Longmans and Green,
1827), another edition of which came out in Paris in 1828. *The Poetical Works of
William Wordsworth* had been published in four volumes by Cummings, Hilliard and
Company, Boston, in 1824.

[10] A brief review of Wordsworth's *Poems in Two Volumes* (1807) was sandwiched
between enthusiastic notices of the late Mrs. Mary Robinson's *Poetical Works* and
Amelia Opie's *Warrior's Return* .... Wordsworth's *Poems* were dismissed by the
reviewer, who had never seen anything "better calculated to excite disgust and anger
in a lover of poetry", as "drivelling nonsense". See *The Poetical Register and Re-
spository of Fugitive Poetry,* VI, (1811), 540-41.
    When *Peter Bell, A Tale in Verse* was printed in 1819, a reviewer asked: "Can
Englishmen write, and Englishmen read, such drivel, such daudling, impotent drivel, — as this . . . ?" See *The Monthly Review,* LXXXIX (August, 1819), 421, or Elsie
Smith's *Estimate,* p. 303,

self, a language sufficient to the heights and depths of all philosophy, and more subtle and powerful in expressing the most delicate and complex shades of feeling, than any English writer
whatsoever, Shakespeare alone excepted. At the same time the
habitual use of an uninflated phraseology gives extraordinary
vigour to all that homely illustration, and fresh, natural imagery,
which are so conspicuous in Wordsworth's poems.[11] But in general his sonnets,[12] the larger number of his minor poems, the
White Doe of Rylstone [1807], and the *Excursion* [1814], are
by no means marked with the lowliness of diction which it is so
common to dwell upon and to ridicule. We find still vigorous in
these poems, and in none but them and the works of Coleridge
and of Shelley, the full harmony and profusion, the swell and
force of our English tongue, the green old age of that majestic
speech in which Spenser wrote the *Fairie Queene* [1589], and
Milton discoursed the *Areopagitica*[13] to angels, to men, and to
eternity.

Connected with this charge is that of Mr. Wordsworth's propensity to represent as his heroes obscure, and therefore uninteresting, personages. But is there or is there not, in the hearts of
men, that true catholic faith in our nature from which we learn
that what interests and engages all our better, and therefore all
our stronger feelings, is not the accidental peculiarity of circumstances, but the immoveable foundations of human being, and its
incorporeal indivisible essence? Place these where you will, so
that they show themselves through the accidental accom-
paniments and are not stifled by them, there is in them that
which draws us to itself and makes us feel the stirrings of kindred
pulses.

But how generally, among the instructed classes, is every free
emotion checked or masked! Sympathy is called affectation;
earnestness, enthusiasm; religion, fanaticism; and the whole of
society beaten down and shrunk into flat barrenness. But among
the ranks of men which are less subjected to fashion, there are
still to be seen yearnings and ebullitions of natural feeling, and
among them mankind may be studied with more accuracy, and
examples of deeper and truer interest discovered, than in the

[11] This paragraph elucidates Wordsworth's Preface.

[12] *The River Duddon* (1820) and *Ecclesiastical Sonnets* (1822), a series of sonnets.

[13] Milton's noblest tract, arguing in 1644 for the liberty of unlicensed printing.

portion to which we belong.

Acting upon this belief, Wordsworth has done more than any-one who has written in our language for two centuries, to realize and bring home to our minds the character of the larger portion of our species. At a time when the favourite personages of even our best poets were Celadons and Musidoras,[14] when poetry confined itself either to gentlemen and ladies, or to the shadowy indiscriminate mockeries of humanity, the swains of pastoral absurdity — it was doing a mighty service to society to represent the artisan and the peasant even with the external minuteness of Crabbe [1754-1832].

We all feel, nevertheless, that he has looked upon the poor, the uninstructed, and the despised, with an eye rather to the peculi-arities of the individual and the class; and that he has often neglected those things which belong not to classes or to individ-uals, but to mankind — the original and still undiminished inher-itance of glorious hopes and divine faculties. But it is Words-worth almost alone who has shown us how precious are the associations connected with the foot-print of the clouted shoe.

He who paints to us the differences of manners and habits between ourselves and the mass of men, who brings into the strongest light the contrast between stars, lawn-sleeves, and epau-lettes on the one hand, and smock-frocks and checked shirts on the other, does much towards making us conceive of weavers and ploughmen as living and busy beings; instead of leaving us to think of stage figurants in pink-hats and lemon-coloured breeches with gilded crooks and jingling tambourines. But how infinitely more is done to compel our best sympathies, when herdsmen and pedlars are presented to us not only breathing the breath of the same existence and treading the same green earth as we but, in their different degrees, thinking similar thoughts, agitated by like passions and misgivings, thrilled by kindred impulses of love, joying in the universal presence of one essential beauty, and feel-ing within them and pouring abroad over the world for their own contemplation the power and tenderness of that spirit who lives as strongly in the chalet of the mountaineer, and in the sod-built hut, as among primates, and kaisers, and the conclaves of em-blazoned aristocracies.

This has been done by Wordsworth; and the immortal writings which have been the instruments and fruits of his labour, afford

[14]Light-weight, pastel characters created to appeal to fashionable society.

an admirable illustration of the mode in which it is really useful and wise to combat the evil cause of privileged monopolies and unchristian sectarianism. It is the effect of almost all his works to make men look within for those things in which they agree, instead of looking without for those in which they differ, and to turn to that one source of universal harmony which consists, not in the adoption of the same dogmas or the establishment of the same forms, but in the powers and the tendencies that belong alike to all, that are in communion with the divine nature, and constitute the humanity that distinguishes us from meaner animals. It is this propensity to look at man as an object of affectionate interest independently of any lowliness of station, except in so far as the external circumstances may have influenced the general development of the character, which would commonly be referred to as the greatest and worst peculiarity of Wordsworth. But it is in truth so intimately connected with the general tendencies of his mind and spirit of his philosophy, that it is impossible to refer to it without advocating or opposing all those principles which guide his mode of treating other matters. His general intention obviously is to view all existence as actuated by a single purport, and parts of one great harmony.[15]

But in the present state of society, whatever men may say, the points to which almost everybody attaches a feeling of importance are those which derive an interest from being mixed up with our own individual selfishness. We do not trouble ourselves about the poor for, thanks to the vagrant act and the standing army they are kept pretty much out of our way. We laugh at the law against cruelty to animals because it would not be consistent in fox-hunters and lovers of luxurious eating to care for a little superfluous suffering among oxen and cart-horses. We make speeches in praise of steam-engines and commercial competition, for without these sources of happiness and virtue, where should we get our comforts and splendours? But we shut our ears to the gasping of decrepit children in the stifling atmosphere of cotton-mills, and turn away with carelessness from the flood of debasement and misery which rolls along our streets and overflows into our prisons; while we talk with veneration, the deeper as being indicated rather than expressed, of great capitalists and monied interests.[16]

[15] Wordsworth is a powerful force for social unity.

[16] Contemporary society, beset by competition, is selfish and self-destructive.

Luther is a fanatic and Milton a visionary, because the recollection of unselfish zeal is oppressive to the barren littleness, and troublesome to the fat indolence of the age: and to sacrifice any worldly advantage from love either to God or our neighbour is extravagant folly; for it is not required either by the laws or by public opinion. Thus it is that the vulgar uniformly condemn as absurd any attempt to act from higher motives or with wider views than they do; and therefore are the hearts of most men as hard as the nether mill-stone to the perception of the vast and glorious unity of design and feeling, at once the object and the fruit of that divine presence in which the universe lives and moves and has its being.

Wordsworth has done immensely more than any English writer of modern times to correct this narrowness and meagreness of feeling. He has seen that even though the men and women of instructed society, or the rude warriors of the Middle Ages, the heroes of ancient Greece, or the ruffians of modern Turkey, are in themselves perhaps as good materials for poetry as the peasant poor of Cumberland; yet we are prone enough to sympathise with the former classes, and when their thoughts and actions are covered by writers with a varnish of refinement, to deify misanthropy and fall in love with pollution; but that our affections are cold and dead towards the lowly and the despised, the men who compose the mass of every nation, not arrayed in the renown of splendid crimes; not carried on through a long and uniform career by one absorbing passion; not beings of exaggerated impulses and gigantic efforts; but frail and erring, misguided by vulgar hopes, and grasping eagerly at momentary objects.

We are ready enough to allow that wisdom is treasured up in books; that the thoughts and deeds of the wise and powerful are fit subjects of contemplation; to pour forth our souls in delight at the aspect of armed and towered cities; and to give out the inmost heart of admiration, when we see the thronging armadas of an empire spring forward like the eagle of the deity, to sail before the tempest and bear the thunder round the globe. We rejoice in the goodliness of our own imaginations, and boast ourselves in the might of our own hands.

But it is Wordsworth, and such as Wordsworth, who withdraw us from these exultations to feel the beauty of a pebble or a leaf; to listen to the still small voice which whispers along the twilight streamlet, and murmurs in the sea-side shell; and to lift among the stars a hymn of humble thanksgiving from the crags of lonely mountains. The exuberant sympathies of the poet gush out on every grain of sand; they find a germ of love in every wild-flower of the solitude; they go forth conquering and to conquer, to meet with matter and support even in the dim corners and far wildernesses of creation; but they have their most congenial objects wherever there is a human heart which the poet may speak to in the tone of a kinsman, and find in it a home for his affections.

These peculiarities of Mr. Wordsworth's mind, as displayed in his writings, spring partly from the essential individuality of his nature, and partly from those tendencies of the time which he has wisely thought himself called on to oppose. The succession of men of pure and lofty genius is, indeed, a kind of compensation-balance to society; counteracting alike the opposite extremes of its moral temperature. To the demands of this the appointed office of great men, we may in some degree refer one of the especial points of interest in Mr. Wordsworth's disposition and powers.

He seems to have scarcely any propensity to increase his knowledge or sharpen his apprehension of the every-day doings of worldly men. He loves to repose upon meditation, or only to send forth the mind for the purpose of contemplating the beauty of the material world, or of studying man in the individual; instead of mingling actively with the busy life of society. He pours into his personages the strong life and moving breath of genius, but they have little of the air of the mart or the farm-yard. They have, indeed, all that which is so completely wanting in the heroes of Lord Byron, the absolute truth of being, the nature which is so uniform under so many varieties; they are made up of the elements of universal, but want the accidents of social, humanity.

Wordsworth appears to take no pleasure in watching the entangled threads of passion which bind together crowds with such many-coloured, yet scarcely distinguishable feelings. He retires from the conflict of mingled and heterogeneous interests. He loves to muse by winding rivers; but the tumultuous current of men's ordinary motives has little for his contemplation. He delights to gaze upon cities; but it is when "all that mighty heart is lying still." He cares not to trace through all the eagerness of men's selfish pursuits, a subtle vein of better feeling; or to look with keen and searching eye upon the follies and fluctuations of society. He has, therefore, no dramatic power whatsoever, and would probably fail completely in the simplest form of tragedy; while comedy is entirely out of the question.

In all this he is directly the opposite of his greatest contemporary poet, Goethe, who seems to take almost equal pleasure in the study of every class of human character, and to delight in tracing the involutions of cunning or the rush of crime; at least as much as in observing and sympathizing with pure and lofty excellence. Goethe, moreover, is peculiarly shrewd and philosophical in detecting the action and reaction of social circumstances on individual character, the intertwining of good and evil motive, and the most delicate and apparently causeless shades of capricious selfishness. The difference of the two minds is perhaps wisely ordained. For the practical and working Englishman will be benefited and improved by those aspirations to invisible good and inward perfection, towards which the Germans are already far more generally inclined. Whether the German is or is not too abstracted a being, may admit of dispute; but there can be little doubt that the Englishman is vastly too much engrossed with the casual business of the hour. His thinking is far too completely guided by the multiplication-table and the foot-rule.

This fondness for the actual and the outward, this tendency to wrap ourselves up in the petty interest of the moment, is opposed by the whole strain of Wordsworth's poetry. He diffuses his affections over everything around him; and lets them be restricted by no arbitrary limits, and confined within no sectarian enclosures. He looks round upon the world and upon man with eyes of serene rejoicing; and traces all the workings of that spirit of good, of whose influence he is conscious in his own heart.

But from his want of that mastery over forms which was never possessed so perfectly by anyone as by Shakespeare, he cannot make so intelligible to all men, as he otherwise might, the depth and value of his own feelings. This has prevented his works from becoming more powerful instruments than they can for ages be, in diffusing the free philosophy and catholic religion so conspicuous throughout his writings.

For those, however, who really wish to understand the mind, and sympathise with the affections of this glorious poet, there is nothing in his works of rugged or ungrateful. The language is the most translucent of atmospheres for the thought. The illustrations are furnished by a sensibility of perception which has made his memory a store-house of substantial riches. The images are moreover the types of none but the truest and most healthy

feelings; and the ethics of this most philosophical Christian may
all be summed up in the one principle of love to God and to his
creatures. Like those angels who are made a flame of fire, he
burns with a calm and holy light, and the radiance which shows
so strange amid the contrasted glare and blackness of the present,
will blend with the dawning of a better time as with its native
substance

SKETCH VI

Mr. Moore[1]

Why is it that Ireland has not produced a great poet?[2] According to the vulgar estimate of what is necessary to poetry, that country ought to have been peculiarly fertile in it. Irishmen are proverbial for strong, quick feeling, and rich fancy: yet we believe there are few persons who would maintain that Ireland has ever had a first-rate poet. It has always, in truth, been so ill-governed that the national mind has never reached those "regions mild of calm and serene air", in which is the domain of ideal beauty. It has never been so relieved from the pressure of the present, as to gain for its intellect a sufficient comprehension of the eternal which includes in itself the past and the future. It has never been so much lightened of the load of outward objects, as that its imagination could learn to wield them with a majestic omnipotence as the symbols and interpreters of universal principles. Its feelings have been kept in a state of perpetual irritation, and have not been allowed to concentrate themselves into that quiet strength which is necessary for the purpose of embracing Truth and Good. Ireland has, therefore, no great speculative, historical, or poetical writers: in one word, it has no philosophers: — orators and novelists it has: for the qualities it wants are precisely those required to produce the higher excellencies whereby the poem is distinguished from the romance, and the history from the speech.

Mr. Moore is the writer who would be cited, if any were, as a contradiction to our statement that Ireland has never nourished a great poet. But there are so many substantial reasons against his claim that it is not difficult to show its insufficiency. His poems

---

[1] *Athenaeum* (22 February 1828). Thomas Moore (1779-1852), close friend and biographer of Byron, published his first volume of poetry under the pseudonym, Thomas Little.

   Maurice reveals the Coleridgean "torch of guidance", the basis of his philosophical criticism, in this sketch (VI, 12).

[2] Maurice is writing fifty years before Yeats.

are deficient in the first great requisite, that which ought to be the groundwork or, as it were, the very spirit of their beauty — truth.

If we look merely at their imagery, at the pictures of outward objects which they display to us, it is clear that in this they are found wanting. It is not that he regards them through a differently-coloured atmosphere, or on a different side, from other men; but that he studiously and elaborately represents them in a way in which no one ever saw them. It is not that he brings them too near him by a telescope, or examines them too much in detail with a microscope, or uses spectacles of green or purple, or looks at the landscape through a pictured window of a thousand different colours, or dims the glory of the sun by a smoky glass; but his very eye seems facet-cut, made up of innumerable different angles and surfaces — here refracting a ray, and there reflecting the corner of an object, so that he perceives no consistent or permanent appearance whatsoever, but lives in a universe of sparkling points and fragments and wanders on from delusion to delusion. He never gives us a representation of what is; but as if the world had sometime or other in its childhood chosen to put itself into masquerade, and he had since got possession of the cast-off finery, he arrays it anew in the tarnished tinsel and old artificial flowers and pompously exhibits it as if in mockery of things as they are.

Everyone must have observed that when we are placed in some accidental position, a bit of quartz or glass upon an open bank or distant hill will catch the rays of the sun and shine with a dazzling brightness. If Mr. Moore were describing the landscape in which this had occurred to him, he would omit the broad blue sky, the fields, the forests, the mountain, and the lake, to dwell upon and exaggerate this momentary and casual triviality, to illustrate it by a thousand pretty images, and expand it into a galaxy of splendour. His fancy never looks abroad to great view; his mind always fixes upon some petty salient point, instead of the whole. To get a notion of the heavens, it follows the zig-zag flight of a butterfly; and rather than contemplate the teeming profusion of the earth, in the general, it would hunt out some single snail and then grow witty about a Frenchman's dinner, or Lord Eldon's decisions.[3]

In this respect, he and a Chinese painter are specimens of

[3] John Scott, first Earl of Eldon (1751-1838), famous for the delay of his court.

contrasted errors. The one delineates on his jars and screens only a part of what he sees, but frequently gives that part with amazing fidelity; though omitting, to be sure, the light and shade, perspective, expression, and so forth. Mr. Moore adds to everything he sees something of his own; which is not only shown so prominently as to throw into the background whatever scrap or angle of truth there might at first have been, but which is also utterly inconsistent with it.

But not merely is it true that he does not represent to us the outward world in its natural simplicity but, what is of infinitely more importance, he disguises human nature. He tries to improve it into prettiness, to varnish it into a sort of ball-room elegance; and being a person of great talent, succeeds in the attempt better than almost anyone we could name. But this is a slender consolation. The thoughts in his poems are not our thoughts; nor his feelings, our feelings. They are not those that ever could occur to anyone in the situations he represents; they are not those that would occur to himself. It will be said, however, — Where did he get them, if they were not the natural products of his own mind? We answer, they were not its natural, but its artificial products; obtained not by art, but by artifice. If an opera-dancer exhibits himself looking over a battlement, he does not stand as it would be his unconscious impulse to stand supposing nobody were to see him; but he stretches out his hands, simpers, and performs a pirouette. So it is with Mr. Moore; instead of looking round him quietly, he simpers and pirouettes.

It is obvious that there ought to be nothing in poetry which might not be the spontaneous outgrowth of the human mind in some one state of feeling or other; and this, for the plain reason that it is human nature, or its qualities in some other shape, with which the poet intends us to sympathise. Now, if, as is commonly the case with Mr. Moore's works, a part of the sentiment be really such as might exist in the mind under the supposed circumstances, and part such as could only occur to an author thinking in the eye of the public, our feelings are continually withdrawn from the personage designed to be brought before us, and are distracted and dissipated by the inconsistency. We may make our meaning more clear by an illustration. One of the most beautiful of the Irish melodies is as follows:

I saw thy form in youthful prime,
  Nor thought that pale decay
Would steal before the steps of time,
  And waste its bloom away, Mary!
Yet still thy features wore that light
  Which fleets not with the breath;
And life ne'er looked more purely bright
  Than in thy smile of death, Mary!

As streams that run o'er golden mines,
  With modest murmur glide,
Nor seem to know the wealth that shines
  Within their gentle tide, Mary!
So, veiled beneath a simple guise,
  Thy radiant genius shone,
And that which charmed all other eyes,
  Seemed worthless in thy own, Mary!

If souls could always dwell above,
  Thou ne'er hadst left that sphere;
Or, could we keep the souls we love,
  We ne'er had lost thee here, Mary!
Though many a gifted mind we meet,
  Though fairest forms we see;
To live with them is far less sweet,
  Than to remember thee, Mary![4]

The second of these stanzas is as exquisitely finished and as melodious as either of the others; but the thought is fundamentally inappropriate; for no one, lamenting over the grave of youthful loveliness, would think of the distant ingenuity of "The streams that run o'er golden mines". It immediately recalls us from the mourner to the author, and there is an end of our sympathy; yet this is by no means one of the worst among innumerable instances of the same kind in Mr. Moore's poetry. The greatest evil of such passages is that they are faults with the semblance of excellencies; like the ladies who are said to be fond of going to masquerades in the disguise of nuns and vestal virgins.

[4] "Irish Melodies", Section IV, the title being the first line of the poem, *The Poetical Works of Thomas Moore*, (1876). *Yet humbly, calmly glide* is a variant rendering of the second verse of stanza two.

There is, nevertheless, in Mr. Moore's writings, considerably more of genuine feeling and sincere thought than can be discovered at first sight; and to this, together with the factitious merit of their connection with music, must be attributed all their chance of permanent estimation. But, unfortunately, his habit of exaggerating everything he describes and of covering his personages, like the pasteboard figures of our childhood, with the glitter of powdered glass, runs so completely throughout his works and mind that his occasional fragments of single and direct expression are always disguised in turns, and points, and prettiness. He has some of the gold of Ophir,[5] but he is never satisfied without concealing it under French pinchbeck.

Our readers have doubtless seen cathedrals in which the delicate taste of some fashionable dean or refined canon had ornamented marble tombs and airy tracery with a coat of whitewash; and if we remember rightly, the bust of Shakespeare has received more than one layer of paint and varnish. So does Mr. Moore with his ideas. There are beneath the outer frippery many of the lineaments of the true poet. He hides his really graceful ringlets with false curls and artificial love-locks; and daubs over the living hues of health with blotches of white-lead and rose-pink. An Eastern Prince, having obtained a cast of the Medicean Venus,[6] clothed it in the brocades of his favourite Sultana. The barbarians admired; the judicious traveller, though at the risk of his head, burst out into laughter.

There are innumerable persons, and more especially the lovers of music, who will compare his estimate of Mr. Moore with their own consciousness of enjoyment derived from his poetry. To these we shall appear in the light of rugged Vandals, without any taste for elegance or sympathy for refined feeling; but we may, perhaps, partly re-establish ourselves in the favour of our fair and gentle readers by allowing that there really is, in the writings of their pet poet, a great deal of delicate tenderness and polished vivacity. In many of his shorter poems, where we have not time to grow weary of his constant succession of sparkling fire-works, he is one of the most delightful of writers. Even in his most fantastic evolutions he is always graceful; and we acknowledge

---

[5] Mentioned in the Old Testament as a region of uncertain locality whence fine gold was obtained.

[6] Formerly belonging to the Medici family, the statue of the Greek goddess of love and beauty is now in the Uffizi gallery, Florence.

that, though not, like his friend Lord Byron, the Kehama of poetry,[7] he is the most perfect and agile of Indian jugglers. The greatest mischief is that others, who have none of his merits, in attempting to steal from him steal only his defects. Thus, when, in the decline of the Roman empire and of the fine arts, the figures of the deities were adorned with robes and jewels, the wife of Stilicho[8] robbed the image of Vesta of its trinkets, but left behind the statue of the mighty goddess.

His wit, his festive merriment, his graceful feeling, and occasional strength of passion are undeniable merits. But it will be allowed, even by his chief admirers, that something is wanting in the midst of all these. His joyousness is scarcely the rich and happy laughing of the heart which is the only healthy kind of merriment. It has almost always a character either sensual or scornful, and leaves behind no consoling sense of permanent invigoration.

Read any, the most pleasant and mirthful of Mr. Moore's compositions, and then turn to the gladness of Milton's L'Allegro [1632], and the difference is at once perceived. Our feelings are as distinct in the two cases as are those of the guests during the wearisome excitement and glare of a festival, from those of a throng of children playing and rolling about among the primroses of a green and sunny meadow. His witticisms are commonly like icicles, cold, pointed, and glittering. They have none of the racy strength of Irish humour, and resemble far more the repartees of Rochester or Sheridan than those of Shakespeare, the jokes of Voltaire than those of Cervantes.[9]

The tenderness, which is unquestionably to be found in many parts of his works, is almost always unhappily mingled with some frivolous affectation, some fictitious caprice of fancy, which

[7]Kehama, a mighty Raja, pronounced a curse upon Ladurlad, a peasant whose daughter's virginity was threatened by the son of the Raja. The curse ultimately redounds upon the head of its utterer for, because of it, Ladurlad is enabled to save his daughter, while Kehama becomes the fourth supporter of Yamen, the lord of hell. The implications for Byron, the Kehama of poetry, are clear! See Southey's poem, The Curse of Kehama.

[8]Flavius Stilicho (359-408), a Roman governor and general whose wife, Serena, was a niece of the Emperor Theodosius. Vesta was the Roman goddess of the hearth.

[9]John Wilmot, second Earl of Rochester (1648-80), handsome favourite of Charles II, libertine, poet and wit, and Richard Brinsley Sheridan (1751-1816). The humour of The Rivals and The School for Scandal is particular and topical, whereas that of Shakespeare and Cervantes with his seminal burlesque novel Don Quixote de la Mancha (1605) is universal.

never grew out of the heart and never can affect it. His heroes and heroines remind us of some fanciful arabesques, or of his own Irish harp, in which a face of human beauty and a breast that might well be the abode of human feelings, are united to a quaint complication of leaves, and volutes, and gilded tendrils. His passion again, hot and earnest as it sometimes is, loses immensely of its effect by being surrounded, like the flame of the safety-lamp,[10] by a network of delicate subtlety which cuts it off from all around.

The most powerful lines, perhaps, which he has ever written are an execration of the conduct of the Neapolitans for yielding to the Austrians.[11] Yet even in these, which are marked throughout by the most extreme intensity, it is impossible not to feel how much the strength of the poem is weakened by the elaborate ingenuity of the expression. Mr. Moore probably could not write otherwise if he would, and does not perceive the inferiority of his own style to that of the real lords of song. He is not likely to know that poetry abdicates its throne and lays aside its glory, when it draws the materials of the ideal, not from the existing or the possible, but from the limbo of vanity of an unfaithful fancy.

But those who would aspire to a height which he has not attained, should know, as an ever-attendant truth and living presence, the conviction that it is the holy task of the poet to exalt and to purify human nature by the aid of its own, not of extraneous principles, and to imitate the craftsman of the forge, who frames from the rude iron the cunning tools wherewith he may afterwards construct from the same material a panoply of impenetrable strength. Mr. Moore is not likely to learn this from any consideration of general laws; but we imagine that he might be taught to see the inferiority of his own sphere of thought by comparing the fate of similar writers to himself with that of those who have risen into a more elevated region.

Without going to the literature of Italy or Spain, which would furnish us with ample illustration, and omitting that of France which, as containing no poetry, would furnish us with no example of our meaning, let us look merely at our own country, and let Mr. Moore consider the difference between the reputation

---

[10]Invented by Sir Humphrey Davy (1778-1829), friend of Sir Walter Scott and author of *Salmonia, or Days of Fly-fishing* (1828).

[11]Neapolitan air, *Where Shall We Bury our Shame!*

of Cowley and that of Milton.[12] Such as the former clever writer
is, when compared to the latter master poet; such is Mr. Moore,
when weighed against Wordsworth; and such will be the difference of their estimation by our posterity. And in saying this, we
are willing to throw out of the question the *Excursion* which Mr.
Moore has produced nothing to rival; but we would put against
any, the most perfect song he has even written, the lines beginning *She was a phantom of delight*;[13] or, for he has more than
one superior among living poets, Mr. Coleridge's exquisite
stanzas, entitled *Love,* but better known, we believe, by the
name of *Genevieve.*[14]

We have hitherto spoken chiefly of Mr. Moore's serious poetry.
His comic verses, which are mostly political, are certainly inimitable satires. There is in them an ease, a pointedness, a vigour, an
unfailing flow of wit, which our language has scarcely ever
equalled. He wants the terse, quaint couplets of *Hudibras,*[15] and
the blasting energy of Churchill;[16] but for lively sharpness, and
even apt simplicity of expression, he has certainly surpassed
everyone we remember, except Pope [1688-1744]. The age has
done him injustice in treating his odes and tales as of more importance than his political squibs. It is in these that he is really

[12] Abraham Cowley (1618-67) and John Milton (1608-74). In this sentence and with
these names Maurice announces the source of his critical criteria. In *Biographia
Literaria,* i, 62, Coleridge wrote: "Milton had a highly *imaginative,* Cowley a very
fanciful mind. If therefore I should succeed in establishing the actual existence of
two faculties generally different, the nomenclature would be at once determined. To
the faculty by which I had characterized Milton, we should confine the term *imagination;* while the other would be contradistinguished as *fancy.* Now were it once
fully ascertained, that this division is no less grounded in nature ... the theory of
the fine arts, and of poetry in particular, could not, I thought, but derive some
additional and important light. It would in its immediate effects furnish a torch of
guidance to the philosophical critic; and ultimately to the poet himself."

[13] Written in 1804 to Mary Hutchinson, Wordsworth's wife.

[14] In the second edition of Lyrical Ballads (2 vols., 1800), *Love* was a significant
addition to the first volume, the poems of which were substantially those of the
1798 edition. This poem "with four preliminary and three concluding stanzas" had
been printed in the *Morning Post* (21 December 1799) under the title, *Introduction
to the Tale of the Dark Ladie* and, like *The Ancient Mariner* and *Christabel,* was
meant to illustrate "that willing suspension of disbelief ... which constitutes poetic
faith". See *Lyrical Ballads,* edited by R. L. Brett and A. R. Jones (1963), pp. 3, 297;
Collected Letters of Samuel Taylor Coleridge, edited by Earl Leslie Griggs (1966), i,
550; and *Biographia Literaria,* ii, 6.

[15] The mock-heroic, satirical poem by Samuel Butler, modelled on *Don Quixote* and
published in 1663.

[16] Charles Churchill (1731-64) wrote *The Ghost,* a Hudibrastic poem.

unmatchable; while his metrical romance will be considered as a mere elegant curiosity and, as a song-writer, he will occupy an inferior place to Burns and Béranger.[17] The *Two-penny Post-bag*[18] and the *Fudge Family*[19] will be remembered and liked as long as men retain their affection for wit; and yet we doubt whether many pages of these brilliant satires could be read without a sense of weariness and exhaustion. There is also another little book, the *Fables for the Holy Alliance,* and *Rhymes on the Road,*[20] which was received with far less enthusiasm and yet deserves, we think, in some respects, a higher reputation than the former volumes. There is in all of these a freshness and brightness which almost tempt us to wish that the slavery of the world might continue for ever, provided Mr. Moore would for ever write about it as freely as he does at present.

The prose works of this distinguished man are characterised by nearly the same peculiarities as his metrical writings. The perpetual repetition of the same style of ingenious imagery, drawn not from observation but fancy, the polishing away of sentences till they are made to express the smallest possible quantity of meaning, the elaborate melody and finish of every period, and the want of general design and toning in the whole, the light butterfly flippancy, and exaggerated delicacy of sentiment — these are all found in equal prominence in *Little's Poems,* and the *Epicurean* [1827], in his first verses, and his last prose. The unmetrical part of *Lalla Rookh*[21] is by much his best production of this sort. Indeed, we will not hesitate to say that it is one of the most perfect tales in the language. Relieved as it is by the stronger passion of the poetry, we are content to read it as eminently airy and graceful; and to allow for its shallowness of feeling and meagreness of thought. *Captain Rock*[22] is to the full as clever; but we confess that we are pained at seeing the wrongs of a nation

[17] Jean Pierre de Beranger (1780-1857), a popular romance song-writer, a French equivalent of Thomas Moore.

[18] A collection of satires against the Regent, *Intercepted Letters; or, The Twopenny Postbag* . . . . (1813), was edited by Thomas Brown the Younger, a pseudonym of Thomas Moore.

[19] *The Fudge Family in Paris* (1818), also edited by Thomas Brown the Younger.

[20] *Fables for the Holy Alliance, Rhymes on the Road* (1823).

[21] *Lalla Rookh, An Oriental Romance* (1817).

[22] *Memoirs of Captain Rock* (1824).

advocated in a tone of ribaldry which might have become a Provençal Court of Love, or the drawing-room of Madame Du Deffand.[23] Of *The Life of Sheridan* [1825] we had rather say as little as possible; for we look upon it as an attempt, wretched even in the execution, to varnish and vamp into respectability the reputation of a particularly useless, worthless, and heartless wit.

Mr. Moore is not a man who produces any effect upon the world. He is not master of the circumstances of the age; but himself one of them. His politics have a dashing air of liberalism; but his dislikes and affections cling not to things, but names. He does not so much hate bad government, as the particular form of bad government which happens to come directly in his way, and which it is his humour to rail at. He therefore seems to care very little as to what ought to be substituted for existing corruptions, and sees the world's chance of happiness, not in principles, but in the honour and distinction of some of his aristocratic friends.

It is to Ireland that he has principally endeavoured to do good. Yet we much doubt whether, in surrounding that wretched country with a vague halo of fancy, he has not rather taught men to consider its substantial and degrading evils as melodramatic misfortunes, fit subjects for modern sentiment and old quotation, than as the deep-felt and agonizing sufferings of millions of living men. Everything he has written would prove, however, that he is really attached to the cause of Ireland; and great part of what is least satisfactory in his mode of treating its miseries results, no doubt, from the national habit of viewing them rather as matter for metaphor, than constraining occasions of sober and earnest exertion.

[23] An eighteenth-century Parisian literary socialite and hostess.

SKETCH VII

Mr. Brougham[1]

This gentleman is, beyond any question, the most distinguished person in the House of Commons.[2] He stands with this importance before the public eye, having all his life been a working barrister, never having been in office, and in spite of some natural disadvantages. It is worth while to consider by what qualities, and in what circumstances, he has attained his present eminence, and in what particulars it consists.

The ordinary subject of marvel with reference to Mr. Brougham is the variety of his powers and attainments: and he is undoubtedly entitled to be considered as an orator, a lawyer, a statesman, an economist, and a person of scientific information. The mind which has thrown itself actively into these various lines of exertion and has earned a just reputation in most of them, though it need not be a mind of the highest character, must obviously be one of no very common stature. And in truth Mr. Brougham is distinguished by several very remarkable qualifications. His class of power is neither that distinguished by reason,[3] nor by imagination.[4] His great peculiarity is energetic feeling.[5]

[1] *Athenaeum* (29 February 1828). Interested in rhetoric, Maurice in this sketch of Henry Peter Brougham (1778-1868) provides a valuable essay on English oratory. "Hours of Idleness: a Series of Poems . . . by Lord Byron, a Minor", *Edinburgh Review*, XI (January, 1808), 285-89, allegedly by Brougham, is thought to have provoked Byron's *English Bards and Scotch Reviewers.*

[2] For twenty years when, in 1830, he became Lord Chancellor and was elevated to the peerage as Baron Brougham and Vaux.

[3] Maurice applies another Coleridgean distinction, that between reason and understanding. Understanding is sensuous, experiential and, in animals, instinctual. "Reason implies all that distinguishes man from the animals." It includes animal understanding plus self-consciousness, but it is essentially supersensuous and sciential, instinct with powers of reflection, comparison, and suspension of judgment. See *Biographia Literaria,* i, 109-10, and Shawcross's notes, p. 250. Maurice, like Coleridge, found the distinction valuable "as a weapon against the empiricists and necessitarians."

[4] The creative imagination.

[5] Sympathy and feeling nurture the imagination.

But as his mind is far more discursive than creative,[6] his feelings habitually display themselves in a dress of logic. He is therefore especially fitted to excel as an orator; and unquestionably the most extraordinary efforts of his talents are rhetorical. He is deficient in no one of the abilities necessary to eloquence, and possesses many of them in the highest perfection. He has of wit abundance, of fancy enough, both ingenuity and vigour of argumentation, and a quickness and strength of sarcasm, overpowering and tremendous.

His greatest defect is merely of style. It is extremely difficult in the present age to select a phraseology for oratory; as the rich and masculine language of our earlier literature has fallen into neglect, and would scarcely be intelligible, and the meagre poverty of our customary diction is utterly insufficient to large purposes or powerful effects. Mr. Brougham has attempted to remedy this difficulty, partly by drawing the materials of his style from the great authors of the seventeenth century, but chiefly by recurring to Greek and Roman writers, from whom he has derived no scanty variety of phrase; sinewy, indeed, and impressive, but scarcely harmonizing very well with the other elements of his language, or sounding very native to English ears.

It is an error, however, into which he has been driven in company with many of the greatest orators of our country. Chatham imitated, and sometimes plundered, Barrow:[7] Burke[8] collected and heaped up his brilliance from almost every accessible storehouse; from older poetry, and modern science, from the libraries of Academe, and the workshops of Sheffield; and Grattan,[9] whose style belongs more peculiarly to his age, was obliged to

---

[6] *Intuitive* is synonymous with *creative* here. Coleridge's quotation *(Biographia Literaria,* i, 109) from Milton is helpful:

> . . . both life, and sense,
> Fancy, and *understanding*; whence the soul
> *Reason* receives, and REASON is her *being,*
> DISCURSIVE or INTUITIVE: discourse
> Is oftest your's, the latter most is our's,
> Differing but in *degree,* in *kind* the same.
> *Paradise Lost,* V, 485-90.

[7] William Pitt (1708-78), first Earl of Chatham; and Isaac Barrow (1630-77), a Master of Trinity College, Cambridge.

[8] Edmund Burke (1729-97), author of *A Philosophical Enquiry into the Origin of Ideas of the Sublime and the Beautiful* (1756).

[9] Henry Grattan (1746-1820), an Irish politician and patriot.

enrich the barrenness of the eighteenth century, with exuberant metaphor, and to point its feebleness with redundant antithesis.

There is even a more striking singularity in Mr. Brougham's eloquence than the words he employs — sentences, namely into which he casts them. They are distinguished by a rugged and broken involution, a careless complication of clauses, which separates them from the periods of everyone else we remember. He seems so full of his subject that when he has got hold of the framework of a sentence, rather than waste time in making another to contain a new portion of meaning, he goes on filling and piling up the first with argument on argument, and image on image, till he makes the whole a mass, resembling a heap of stones and lava from a volcano, half-fused into unity, rough, enormous, and burning. He never throws out a detached proposition, or includes in a simple definite form of words one step of a deduction; but every thought, however narrow in itself, carries with it so much largeness of feeling that it is always accompanied by references to the whole matter which went before or is to follow, either indicated by some historic vividness or prophetic splendour of epithet embraced in some master principle, or insinuated more strongly than by open declaration in some biting or blasting sarcasm.

He coils his interminable sentences around the point at issue, and binds it to his purpose with a thousand chain-like involutions, drawn out, twisted, and tied together. He does not, like Grattan, overthrow his antagonist at a single spring, and then employ himself in mangling the carcass; but he winds his serpent folds round, and round, and round, and combines and interlaces them with each other, crushing a limb with every knot, till by one irresistible compression he forces out the life of his victim. His speeches have no glittering polish, no airy pleasantness — little of gorgeous exhibition or ostentatious subtlety. His playfulness is the sport of a mail-clad soldier and his toys, like those of the Spartans, are weapons of conflict and death. His hand seems little accustomed to the graceful sweep of display, but it is practised to strike right forward at his antagonist; and like that of the old Roman,[10] or of Goethe's Champion,[11] it is rather a hand of

[10] Cicero, author of *De Oratore*.

[11] Faust, who willed not to surrender to Mephistopheles until, conscious of having done a good work for mankind, he wished to prolong the "moment", and pronounced the magic words that released him.

iron than of flesh and blood.

His illustrations are commonly more homely than fanciful. He comes before his audience not from fairy-land, but from the judgement-hall, the manufactory, the hospital, and the farm-yard. He does not seduce us to his object through an enchanted garden; but he drags us along with irresistible power through the streets and the chambers we have been accustomed to traverse or inhabit. The bulk of his speeches consists of impassioned ratioci-nation; but the parts intended especially for display are either fearfully sarcastic — and this is their most usual character — or filled with a grave and lofty declamation, concise, simple, and of an earnest majesty.

He attends little to melody of style, but much to emphasis; and therefore it is that, with all its incorrectness and irregularity, there have been few orators whose productions are less fatiguing either to hear or read; and a speech of Mr. Brougham's appears to us infinitely more effective in all the careless energy with which it is delivered, than if it had been refined and elaborated into a more minute elegance. His want of smoothness and glitter takes nothing from the substantial power of his eloquence; and his scorn of the gayer and more graceful appliances, so dear to Isocrates and Cicero, reminds us of that Lacedemonian Isadas[1][2] who, without waving crest or sparkling shield, conquered by overpowering courage and the naked vigour of his arm.

Such appears to us, in few words, the characteristics of Mr. Brougham's eloquence. It has qualities which entitle it as com-pletely as any modern oratory to high and permanent estimation. But rhetoric, in its own nature, must be calculated for imme-diate, not for future results. All the immense differences between its laws and those of written composition, while they are guides to present success, are bars against prospective reputation. If a speech has all the peculiarities of a good essay, it is a bad speech. If it is essentially oratorical, it is a bad essay; and when it is judged of as an essay, will be found wanting.

Mr. Brougham's eloquence will leave a trail of glory behind it; but by far the greater portion of his future fame will depend upon the purposes for which he has employed it, and the perma-nent traces which it leaves behind in the good it has achieved and instituted. And brilliant as is the name he has won by his oratory, there are still nobler titles to honour in many of the objects to

[1][2] Like Cicero, the Greek Isocrates was also a great orator. Though lacking their polish, Brougham has courage comparable with that of the young Spartan of Lacedemonia.

which he has dedicated his powers.

It is the great misfortune of his life that he has been uniformly a partisan. It is at intervals and, as it were, episodically, that he has laboured in other public paths, but it has been the business of his existence to support a political sect, and a sect the more contemptible because chiefly distinguished, not by an adherence to any peculiar set of opinions, but as supported by some great aristocratic families, and clinging to a few obsolete and senseless watchwords. By lending to a faction his powerful name and extraordinary talents, together with all the well-merited influence of his genuine public services, he has done far more than anyone living to strengthen and animate the spirit of party – the spirit which makes men anxious for names and not for things, for men and not for truths, for accidents and not for principles, for pretences and not for realities. He has been fighting, not in a great cause, but for a loud war-cry.

He has subjected himself to that degrading and enfeebling system which teaches us, instead of casting away every restriction and so to run freely, and run all in search of truth, to tie ourselves together like a gang of galley-slaves, and make the very bonds that unite us with each other, but chains that proclaim and compel our servitude. And not only has he done much to strengthen the principle of party, but he has exhibited in his own person a striking instance of its evils. For who, in referring to the history of the last twenty years, and comparing what has been done by Mr. Brougham with the vast questions that have been disputed during his life, can doubt that but for the party by which he has so long been displayed in triumph, a manacled captive, he would have accomplished immensely more of good than almost any other man has had in our day the opportunity of achieving. But this is a painful matter, and one from which, at least for the present, we will turn away.

The salient points of his history are, with hardly an exception, pleasant to think upon. The Queen's trial[13] scarcely involved any of the great political principles at stake among mankind. But it was certainly satisfactory to see Mr. Brougham's abilities employed in defence of a woman who, whether guilty or innocent, was certainly far the least guilty of the two parties in the cause, and who yet would have relieved the greater offender from a

[13] Caroline (1768-1821), Queen Consort of George IV, on trial in the House of Lords for alleged adultery.

restraint, by suffering punishment for her own inferior and, at all events, retaliatory criminality.

There was during, and immediately after, this singular proceeding, a general feeling of something approaching to disappointment at the oratory on both sides. Mr. Brougham's speeches were incomparably the ablest which the occasion drew forth. But the excess of the public interest, and the greatness of the opportunity, overpowered even Mr. Brougham's abilities; and acute and ·splendid as was much of his eloquence, it was, and must have been, inferior to an expectation which knew no indifference and paused not at any limits.

Assembled Greece, which crowded around the bema of Demosthenes at the contest for the crown, must probably have been disappointed, even by that magnificent oration, which still remains to feed our delight and command our astonishment. Let anyone now read over the speeches[14] at the Queen's trial, now when it is scarcely remembered as a distant occurrence and its unhappy object is in the coffin[15] — and there is much of eloquence produced by Mr. Brougham, which will bear comparison with almost any we remember. On some occasions, too, where nothing is to be found recorded that would excite admiration, there was that of inspiration in the look and tone, which gave an amazing power to the simplest expressions — such, for instance, was the case with that sentence, in reply to an application for delay, when bursting from a quiet that looked almost concentrated into marble, he flung his hands above him as if they had been spreading pinions, and exclaimed, "Now, my Lords! are you a Court of Justice?"[16]

His conduct with regard to the Roman Catholic question has been unvarying and admirable; and his great and undeniable popularity is a perfectly decisive refutation of the statement that Emancipation and all its supporters are regarded with horror by the middle classes of England. It is scarcely a thing to be dwelt

---

[14] Brougham's speeches were published in the first instance in pamphlet form, this one being "Mr. Brougham's Speech, in the House of Lords, October 3 and 4, 1820", *Speeches of Mr. Brougham, Mr. Denman, and Dr. Lushington; containing the defence* . . . (1820). But see *Speeches* in *Works of Henry Lord Brougham* (1872), IX, X, and for his defence of the Queen, IX, 77-200.

[15] The Queen died 7 August 1821.

[16] See *A Correct, Full, and Impartial Report, of the Trial of Her Majesty, CAROLINE, Queen Consort of Great Britain before the House of Peers on the Bill of Pains and Penalties,* edited by J. H. Adolphus (1820), p. 326.

upon to Mr. Brougham's praise, that he is an enemy to civil
inequalities on account of religion, for it may be taken for
granted of everyone not a clergyman, who is at all superior in
social wisdom to the mass of mankind. Yet, though we do not
mention it to his praise, it is agreeable to contemplate another
addition to the throng of illustrious names which may be in-
scribed upon the banners of Emancipation. Grattan, Burke, Fox,
Plunket, Canning, and, we are delighted to be able to add,
Chalmers,[17] are men with whom even Mr. Brougham need not be
ashamed to ally himself. The way in which he has always defended this good cause is an admirable contrast to the ruffian and
ignorant violence with which it has sometimes been advocated in
Ireland.

His opposition to the Orders in Council[18] with regard to
American commerce, is another of the bright honours of Mr.
Brougham's career. He displayed on this subject several of the
highest qualities of eloquence, and his speeches may be thought
of with the more satisfaction, because the talents they exhibited
were put forth in opposition to a stupid and mischievous monopoly. We regret that as much cannot be said for all his conduct
with regard to internal as to external policy. The way in which he
has treated the question of reform in Parliament, will be chronicled against his name for ever.[19]

It is peculiarly unwise in Mr. Brougham, according to mere
selfish calculation, that he does not rely more upon the people
and less upon the aristocracy; for he is one of the few public men
we have, who would be perfectly sure of enthusiastic support
from the great mass of the nation. His popularity must be felt as
a perpetual thorn by the powers to whom he belongs, and whom
he has served so constantly; but there is not a plebeian, the
humblest and the most wretched, who has ever heard his name,
that would not receive Mr. Brougham as the friend of the poor,
and the patron of the oppressed; and this not only because he has
frequently stood forward for beneficent objects, but because
there is in all he does an air of sincerity and kindness, a reality of

[17]Charles James Fox (1749-1806), William Conyngham (1770-1854) first Baron
Plunket, George Canning (1770-1827), and Thomas Chalmers (1780-1847) favoured
Catholic emancipation.

[18]Forbidding trade with France and thus a cause of the war with United States.

[19]Maurice is probably referring to the opposition of Brougham and other liberal Tories
to an extension of the franchise in certain unrepresented cities.

sympathy, which is rare among public men, and especially among leaders of parties.

The disposition to concern himself heartily for the good of the people, has been especially displayed in his proposals for reform in the laws. In that long oration which has so lately been delivered,[20] though there is by no means sufficient suggestion of remedies, and the evil is not sought for nearly deep enough; yet the wish to examine and to amend is so clearly displayed, and the general abstinence of a great rhetorician from any needless rhetorical display, is so marked and praiseworthy, that it deserves to be estimated as one of the most valuable speeches ever spoken in the House of Commons.

The infinitely greater extendedness of plan than ever was proposed by Mr. Peel [1788-1860], makes it a farce to consider that person's proceedings as anything more than a useful appendage to Mr. Brougham's, and to those disgracefully frustrated attempts of Sir Samuel Romilly [1757-1818], and Sir James Mackintosh [1761-1832]. The conclusion of the speech in question may be pointed out as a particularly impressive example of eloquence, and one in which the moral sublime of the sentiment was carried as far as would be tolerated in one of the least moral and least sublime assemblies in the world—the English House of Commons.

The wonderful energy of his mind has also shown itself in a very amiable and beneficent light with regard to West India slavery.[21] That disgraceful plague-spot in our empire is preserved from every purifying touch by a barrier of interested power which it is dangerous and almost hopeless to assail. The plain proposition that nothing can give one man a complete and indefeasible right over the will of another, is met by such a complex hostility of ancient prejudice and desperate self-interest, that the man who offers to profane the worship of the monstrous idol set up by these debasers of humanity, deserves to be protected and encouraged by the applause of all good men.

The wretched beings of a different colour from us, who are employed at the other side of the Atlantic in ministering to our luxuries, have so few outward bonds of communion with ourselves, that it is not wonderful the many who have no interest in

[20] A six-hour speech, *Present State of Law,* made in the House on 7 February 1828, a third edition of which was out within the year.

[21] Brougham spoke against slavery and the slave trade on numerous occasions: *Speeches* in *Works* (vols. IX, X).

ameliorating their condition should forget their sufferings, or
that the few who have an interest in preventing improvement,
should continue to tyrannise. But honour and praise be to those
who use the talents God has given them in working charity to his
creatures. And in other times, when schools and churches shall
crown the mountains of Jamaica and the cottage of the Negro
peasant shall be sacred from the brutality of white men, when
the scourge shall no longer sound among the Antilles, nor the
image of God be trampled by the slave-driver into the likeness of
the beasts that perish, the name of Henry Brougham will not be
omitted in the thanksgivings of a redeemed people.

Nor unworthy of being mentioned together with these things
are the exertions of Mr. Brougham for education. First came the
plan for a national system of instruction; then the Mechanics'
Institutes; then the London University;[22] then the Society for
Useful Knowledge. We differ on many points from Mr. Brougham
as to the best mode of education; but who can want esteem, we
had almost said affection, for the man who, under a constant
violence of opposition, has attempted all this, and realized so
much of it. Mr. Brougham, by these various endeavours, has
sought to clear away the clouds and thick darkness which have so
long rested on the land; and to make knowledge an inheritance,
common as the air, to all, instead of its being a precious influence
confined to the selected few.

Happy, indeed, would be the oppressors of mankind if they
could monopolize mental acquirements, like food, or privileges,
or titles, and leave the mass of men as stupid as they are unpro-
tected, and as narrowed in thought as they are restricted in action. But the mind, thank God! is free and open, even though the
hands be chained; and while the evils of our social system have
degraded the great mass of the people of this country, it has been
Mr. Brougham's desire to elevate their intellects from the dust,
and to nourish them into strength by instruction. The Mechanics'
Institutes, and the Society for Useful Knowledge, are admirable
instruments of so excellent a design; but we fear that at least the
latter plan has not been so well executed as we could have
wished.

---

[22]Brougham made a speech in the House as early as 8 May 1818 on the education of
the poor. Founded in 1823, the London Mechanics' Institute, assuming its founder's
name, eventually became Birkbeck College, London University.

The London University[23] attempts another kind of good, and must apparently succeed in accomplishing it. The first idea of this institution was suggested and repeatedly urged by Mr. Campbell; but without the influence and power of Mr. Brougham's assistance, it could not probably have been carried into effect. In supporting such a project he has done a good to his country, which even England could hardly repay. One of the worst and most permanent evils of our condition is the aristocratic and ecclesiastical monopoly of opinion. The only recognised and fashionable means of instruction among us are in the hands of those who have an interest in teaching aristocracy rather than politics, and a creed rather than a religion. This tendency runs through the whole mind of the country, and it must be opposed indirectly by the London University.

Many errors will, in all probability, be taught there, though not so many as in institutions which are, at least to a certain extent, found to stand still while the world is moving forward. And this is in truth the great point, that there shall be nothing to shackle, nothing to detain; that if we do not draw on the age, we may, at least, not hold it back; that if we are not masters, we may at all events be servants to time. It is well to embody knowledge in institutions; but it is well also to remember that an improving and expanding soul must be united for ever to a body which cannot improve or grow; and that if the material portion of man were eternal, it would become a dungeon to the perfected spirit. Death is provided as a remedy for man; but, alas! there is none for the British Constitution or the University of Cambridge.[24]

The kind of education which Mr. Brougham seems fond of, is one which does very much to spread an acquaintance with the exact sciences. The knowledge of the exterior world appears to be in his opinion the most proper object of pursuit, and as far as can be judged from his writings, he would give the mind very little assistance in developing itself, except by putting into it as

[23] The poet, Thomas Campbell (1777-1844) urged the establishment of a liberal college incorporating features both of Scottish and German institutions. Owing largely to Brougham, University College, London, opened its doors in 1828 as an undenominational centre of higher learning with "no religious tests for teachers or taught". For the establishment of King's College under the Church and the subsequent federation of the two in 1836 as the University of London, see F. J. C. Hearnshaw, *The Centenary of King's College 1828-1928* (1929).

[24] Compulsory subscription to the Thirty-nine Articles was abolished at Cambridge in 1856, effective by 1871.

And herein is the fault of his plan of education, that it would imprison the infinite in finite, and subordinate conscience to sense. He derives, as it would seem, the idea of a God from without, and deduces the invisible from the visible; forgetting that it is not through the lower we can know the higher; but that to the higher power the lower existence is manifest. He has not proposed any plan for cultivating more wisely and carefully the better feelings of mankind; but seems to imagine that universal justice may be obtained by chemical analysis, and that benevolence will be the product of a quadratic equation. We regret that his own tastes and habits have led him into so grievous an error; and wide as is the good which must result from merely turning general attention to education, he would have achieved incomparably more of benefit, if he had put forth all the resources and engine of his powerful mind to sweep away the great and desperate delusion that acquaintance with the outward world can satisfy the cravings of the inner man.

But in spite of all which has been left undone by Mr. Brougham, the day must come when mankind will act upon the knowledge that happiness is a feeling, and not an opinion, and virtue a state of the heart, and not of the intellect — a time when it will be the object of our schools and pulpits, our literature and social system, to make men gentle, humble, brave, beneficent and self-denying, and to actuate them by no motives but love to God and man; subduing inquiries, arts, and inventions to be the instruments, not the standards, of good, and seeing more of precious influence in one kindly feeling, one generous sacrifice, than in all the rivalries of colleges, the shadowy limbos of libraries and museums, the quarrels of theologians about "the letter that killeth," and the contempt of worldly men for "the spirit that giveth life."

The errors of Mr. Brougham's system of education connect themselves closely with the general character of his mind. The domain of his affections is the outward; the study of his life has been the positive. His days have been divided between the researches of science, and the contentions of law and government. There is nothing about him of those tendencies to penetrate above that which is accidental and transitory into the region of the necessary and the eternal. His thoughts are not meditative or much as possible of positive instruction from without. If he could, he would make all men natural philosophers. He would give them the habit of measuring the universe with a rule, and weighing it in a balance.

reflective; but active and practical.

He sees what is around him, and impresses himself upon it. But he never attempts to withdraw from the turbulent and eager present, into those regions of purer and more abstract feeling to which the best and wisest natures habitually journey. And it is on this account that, as a mere momentary agent, he is so infinitely less useful than he would otherwise have shown himself. Be it his praise that though, among perfectly unworldly men, he would scarcely find a place, and though, among philosophers he would be held as one who had constantly mistaken the types and shadows of truth for truth itself; yet rank him either among lawyers or statesmen, and he stands forth from the crowd with a loftiness of stature and brightness of glory, which in our day and land have belonged to none beside.

SKETCH VIII

Percy Bysshe Shelley[1]

The nation has been taught, or at least told, to think that the character of Shelley was vitiated by one fundamental error — which debars him at once from being considered as exerting a good moral influence, and by consequence as well as by parity of reasoning, from being held for a great poet — an error which proved him to be both a fool and a villain — the want of belief in religion. We rate, at as high a value as anyone ever has put upon them, those feelings which result from the development of the religious principle in the human mind: but we deny that these feelings did not exist in Shelley; we deny that this principle was not developed; we think that without these feelings, and this development, he could not have been a great poet — but we think just as decidedly that he might have been a good man. To accuse anyone of atheism is an easy way of defeating his claims to intellectual and imaginative power, and moral excellence, when the greater part of society have a very confused notion of what atheism is, but a very strong persuasion that it is something extremely horrible.

By way of making this matter a little clearer than it ordinarily is, we shall spend upon it a few sentences; and we can assure our readers that they need not fear the slightest attempt to depreciate either natural religion or Christianity which form together the glory and consummation of our nature. Atheism is the want of conviction of the existence of a God: and the value of that conviction must depend entirely upon the character assigned to the Deity in the mind of the believer, and habitually present to his feelings. The belief in a Supreme Being is entirely useless when, as is the most common case, he is merely thought of as a vague abstraction dwelling afar off from men; or when, as is frequent among the ignorant and fanatical, he is imaged out as a

---

[1] *Athenaeum* (7 March 1828). In the most lyrical of the *Sketches,* Maurice illuminates Shelley (1792-1822) in a "profusion of metaphor", the only means of limning a mind so gloriously imaginative.

venerable idol seated in the clouds, with hoary locks and a frowning countenance; or when he is considered, as he is by many of the instructed classes, the mere first cause and moving spring of the world's mechanism;[2] or when he is revered as essentially a malignant being who, having power to make men what he pleased, has made the majority of them eternally miserable. It must be evident to all that, under one or other of these shapes alone is God present to the intellects of the greater number of nominal Christians. Yet this worse than unmeaning sound of religion is brought forward as a favourable contrast to the opinions of all those who, instead of professing to believe in a God with none of the attributes that can excite our love, boldly profess that they believe in no existence superior to man.

God is, in truth, the concentration and essence of good, and it is because he is such that the constant feeling of his existence is beneficial to the human mind. But of two persons, neither of whom is conscious of the love of this impersonated excellence, which is in the healthier moral condition: he who delights in all the manifestations of the Divine goodness and attempts to make them the models and principles of his own being, though without referring them to their true original and centre; or he who, with all his word-religion, knowing just as little of a pervading and ruling spirit of beauty, truth, and beneficence, at the same time does not discover in the universe any of that power and harmony which the former sees and loves, only without attributing them to an adequate cause? The one is in the right way, though he has not reached his journey's end. The other has left the road, and either stands still, or wanders farther and farther from the path which leads us to the sanctuary. The one is guided by the pillar of fire though still, perhaps, far from the land of promise; the other is either chasing a meteor or, in hopeless inactivity, lamenting for "the flesh-pots of Egypt".

Wherefore then should it be said that an atheist is necessarily a bad man? He is one in whom the faculty, or part of our nature whereby we see and embrace the Divine idea, is still lying undeveloped; but it may be that as well as he yet sees, he struggles to conform himself to the truth, and to open out into the fullness

[2]Those who see God through Hobbesian eyes: "For seeing life is but a motion of limbs, the beginning whereof is in some principal part within; why may we not say, that all *automata* (engines that move themselves by springs and wheels as doth a watch) have an artificial life? For what is the *heart*, but a *spring*; and the *nerves*, but so many *strings*; and the *joints*, but so many *wheels*, giving motion to the whole body, such as was intended by the artificer?" *Leviathan*, the introduction.

of wisdom, the gleams of knowledge which he already possesses; and above all, why do we, instead of imitating the holy gentleness of Christ, overwhelm with obloquy and persecution those whom our unchristian intolerance may irritate and harden, but never can convert? It is at least as bad to have a degrading and polluted idea of God as to have no idea of him at all, and neither the error nor the defect can be remedied by scorn or indignation.

The very first grounds and conditions necessary towards conceiving the personality of a universal spirit of love are that we ourselves should be imbued with benevolence and truth. And those who are selfish and frivolous, though acknowledging God with their lips or even with their intellects, are infinitely farther from him in their hearts than the atheist himself, who is really earnest in struggling upwards, and zealous for the promotion of human welfare.

But Shelley was not an atheist; at all events, not in the sense in which that word is commonly understood. He was, in spirit and habit of feeling, the most strongly opposed of all men to that philosophy, if philosophy it may be called, which spends itself among physical causes and can find satisfaction in mere phenomena. He uniformly referred, for the reason and the truth of things, to invisible principles within us or without, of which natural appearances are merely the clothing and the shadow; and they who would attempt, by an abuse of language, to give the notion that he ought to be classed with the empirical metaphysicians, or the mere mechanical philosophers, might as well tie the breathing body to the dead carcass, and liken the living wheels of Ezekiel's vision to the wheels of a steam-engine or an orrery; and not only would they give a totally false idea of the general tendency of his works, but they would also falsify his words.[3] It would be absurd to allude to *Queen Mab* [1813], written, we believe, at the age of eighteen (the most extraordinary book that any boy ever produced) and never published with the author's consent; in all his avowed productions that we have seen, there is no denial of the existence of a Supreme Perfection; but there is, on the other hand, a constant inculcation of the doctrine of an all-informing Power, an Essential Wisdom and Benevolence.

The utmost that can be justly and positively asserted against Shelley's religious opinions is that he was not a Christian. But that we may not be slaves to names instead of ministers to truth,

[3] Shelley's philosophy was one of love.

and worshippers of idols rather than principles, it will be worth while to consider for an instant, wherefore he was not a Christian. The points to which he uniformly alludes, as shocking to his feelings and repugnant to his reason, are not those which are chiefly dwelt upon in the New Testament; such as that "love to God and man is the sum and abstract of religion"; that "we ought to love those who hate us"; that "God is love, and that it is in him we live, move, and have our being".

These, which are the grand distinctions of Christianity, were not the points from which Shelley revolted. But he had been early disgusted by bigotry and intolerance; by the tyranny and self-sufficiency of those who corrupt the Gospel with additions hostile to its whole spirit and proclaim that the God, who became man from love to men, is a cruel and revengeful being and will punish even errors of the intellect by an eternity of suffering, without the slightest design of reforming the sinner.[4] These are the unhappy and lamentable doctrines against which Shelley unceasingly lifted up his voice; and it might be a warning to those who think that "the wrath of man worketh the righteousness of God", if they remembered how their exclusiveness, and wanton outraging of humanity disinclined to the very name of their religion one of the most gentle, benevolent, brave, and self-denying beings to be found in all the annals of genius. But in spite even of the prejudice against Christianity, which sprang in Shelley's mind, from his observation of the evils so gratuitously connected with it, his own writings are instinct with an especially and earnestly religious morality; and he seems to have given up his whole being to the cultivation of feelings the very opposite of sensuality or of selfishness, and to have laboured night and day to keep his mind open to truth, and restless for moral improvement.

The charge of irreligion has been alluded to in the outset for the obvious reason that it is one which, in the opinion of many people, would be sufficient, if established, to decide at once that Shelley has no claims to be judged, even in other respects, by ordinary rules, or submitted to an impartial analysis. We now leave that matter to be settled as the good feelings or the bad doctrines of the world may determine; and proceed to say something of the general character of his mind; and we are inclined to

[4]Maurice was dismissed from his professorships in King's College, London, in 1854, because of his opposition to the doctrine of eternal punishment. The Concluding Essay — On Eternal Life and Eternal Death — in his *Theological Essays* (reprinted, 1957), p. 302 ff., treats the subject in some detail.

think it was more fundamentally and uniformly poetical than
that of any other poet, at least in our day. We do not say that he
wrote better poetry than Coleridge or Wordsworth; but that
more habitually than they, or indeed than anyone else we can
remember, he thought and felt poetically.

He cannot be conceived as performing the most ordinary action, and not investing it with a wild gracefulness, or imaginative
splendour. Other men put out their minds into the task of ideal
creation with something of effort and preparation; they bare
their arms for the wrestling, or gird their loins for the combat.
But Shelley seems to have been always and all over poet. He did
not delay to put on armour for the battle; but went forth in the
naked beauty of that form, which was in itself invulnerable, and
with a glory blazing on his brow,

ἀμφὶ δέ οἱ κεφαλῇ νέφος ἔστεφε δῖα θεάων
χρύσεον ἐκ δ᾽ αὐτοῦ δαῖε φλόγν παμφανόωσαν.[5]

His whole being seems to have been absorbed and transfigured
into poetry: and though the sphere of his writings is as different
from "this dim spot, which men call earth", as are the clouds of
sunset from the world, with whose horizon they mingle, yet it is
not a region to which he was borne on the wings of a casual
enthusiasm, but his fatherland and accustomed home. He did not
first look at an object as it seems to other men, and then consider
how it might be represented so as to please in poetry; but his
very perceptions seem to have been modified and exalted by his
genius, and even his senses were inspired. It is on this account
that his poems have such perfect unity of feeling. His labours do
not show those inconsistencies which arise among other men,
from the variable humour and energy of the moment. They are
but a homogeneous fragment of the permanent substance of his
mind. Many may have felt that he has too completely thrown
away the ordinary vestures of human nature, that he may crown
himself with asphodel, and array his limbs in light; but no one
can have mistaken him for an ordinary masker, who assumes

[5]   . . . and around his head
      The glorious goddess wreath'd a golden cloud,
      And from it lighted an all-shining flame.
                                      (*Iliad,* xviii, 205-6)
Shelley is likened to Achilles, upon whose shoulders Pallas Athena "flung her fringed
aegis". The translation is that of Tennyson, "Achilles over the Trench", *Nineteenth
Century,* II (August, 1877), 1-2.

successively a dozen different disguises, and wears none of them as if it were his proper garb.

It is rather a failing than a merit in Shelley's character as a poet, a flaw in the lamp of crystal and ruby which holds the flame of his genius, that he looks at the world with a more restless and impassioned spirit than have the other principal poets. He seems always to be carried along by the whirlwind of a strong conviction that his poetry ought to be made the instrument of moral good, which he evidently had as much at heart as any, the greatest of reformers. There is therefore in it a hot and rushing impetuosity which seems to communicate itself from the poet's mind to the objects with which he is conversing, and makes us feel as if we were borne in the prophet's chariot of fire around the burning ramparts of the universe.[6] He does not look upon nature with the serene and clear-sighted steadiness which would be necessary for the purpose of representing it in all its sincerity; but he "Walks with inward glory crown'd"; and it is through the wavering halo of this glory that he contemplates everything around him.[7]

It is not therefore to all men that he writes; for those who cannot readily betake themselves to any other than their ordinary perceptions or remembrances, who cannot lift themselves above the earth or dwell in the ethereal empyrean, are irritated at failing in the attempt, and at seeing another soar so lightly to regions towards which they never can aspire. The rapidity and distance of his flight is indeed sufficient to render weary or giddy the greater number of readers; but they may be sure that if they have courage and strength to cling to his pinions, he will bear them swiftly among the spheres, and into the most secret splendours of the skies. For his is, in truth, a voice that might sing among the morning stars, and swell the shout of the sons of God, rejoicing over new worlds.

He has analysed the substance of man's nature and of the external world for all that they contain of most potent, and condensed the most strangely or sweetly powerful, or the most morbidly sensitive; and he has thus built up for himself, of wilder feelings and more burning or stormy thoughts, another creation, in which he has substituted for the regular breathings of the nature of which we are the household, the pantings and convul-

---

[6] *Flammatia moenia mundi* — Lucretius. [Maurice's note]

[7] Shelley resembles the sage in his poem, *Stanzas Written in Dejection* (1818), III, 5.

sions of ecstasy or agony. He has concentrated all the rays and intensest colours of beauty into an essential loveliness, wherein his heart has placed its home; and while we see around us a glimmering twilight of good and evil, the sober semi-transparent obscurity of our moral being, he divides the light from the darkness, and pours the one into a focus of unmingled love, wherein his thoughts disport like birds in the radiance of the setting sun, and piles the other into a black and beamless chaos, thronged through all its desolate immensity with blind, imperfect shapes of terror and hatred. Yet he abounds with touches of a delicate and ethereal tenderness; his whole spirit is impregnated with a strong and ennobling faith in the capacities of his kind; he brings us within the grasp of a most fantastic and irresistible, but of no degrading or uncelestial, destiny.[8] Though checked, as is the condition of our existence, with many misgivings, weakened by aimless irresolutions, and depressed by doubts and sufferings, he still presents himself struggling on towards the consummation of a mighty hope, and subduing the turbulent revolt of selfishness and passion to the dominion of wisdom and duty.[9] It is from no unintentional profusion of metaphor that Shelley is thus described: but it is impossible without language overswollen by passion, and a crowded array of imagery, to be the limner of a mind in which the imagination was one magnificent hyperbole, and the reason an engine of wondrous powers, overthrowing and piling together the elements of all existence, and rolling, crushing, and labouring under the impulse of an almost terrible excitement.[10]

Of the errors of some of his opinions, taken in their broad and obvious import, few men have had the boldness to profess themselves apologists; and scarce anyone has shown the candour to search among them for valuable, though perhaps lurking, truths. We have already suggested that those of his notions which seem, at first sight, the most awfully mischievous, are frequently erroneous in shape rather than in matter, in expression rather than in

[8]In Coleridgean terms, Maurice is saying that Shelley was "a repetition in [his] finite mind of the eternal act of creation in the infinite I AM", the primary IMAGINATION. Shelley's poetry, "an echo" of this, is the work of his secondary Imagination. See *Biographia Literaria*, i, 202.

[9]The genuine poet exercises a regenerative influence upon society.

[10]Only metaphor and the language of poetry are adequate to describe the true poet. Metaphor, indeed, became the key to Maurice's mode of thought. See *The Conscience* (1868), p. 161.

idea. His affections are the best directed and most generous; his hopes the purest and most elevated. He has never sought to overcome by reasonings any of those primary portions of our nature, on which depend man's moral and spiritual character; and there is no period of human record, no era of uninspired thought, in which this would not have been an uncommon and noble distinction. The muse of his poetry is neither the shadowy phantasm of Greek idolatry, nor a mere earthly "damsel with a dulcimer";[11] but a fair and prophetic priestess in whom the wild gestures, the fire-flushed cheek, and the electric quiverings of every vein and nerve accompany the rapture of no feeble song, and the oracles of no mean inspiration.

There is a close similarity in the modes in which he has treated external nature and the mind of man. He has observed all the most beautiful incidents and appearances in the world around him and he has used them all in his poetry. But he has so brought them together that they crowd upon and encumber each other. He animates them with one spirit, but still there is an excessive accumulation of points to which we are called upon to attend at once.

If a Grecian painter had united, in one face, the brow of Aspasia, the lips of Lais, and the "beaming eye" of Lesbia, supposing he possessed sufficient genius to harmonise their expression, he might have produced a beautiful countenance.[12] But if Phyllis and Chloe[13] happened to have equally well-proportioned noses, and from inability to decide between them, or anxiety to preserve both the fair features on his canvas, he had copied them side by side in the one visage, he would have exhibited not double loveliness, but unexampled deformity. And such is the tendency of Shelley's genius. He often fills his landscape with so many glittering and prominent objects that, though each is separately beautiful, they produce no combined effect whatsoever. Thus he sometimes wearies and dazzles us by heaping together too great a profusion of brilliancies and not producing after all a

---

[11] Coleridge's "damsel with the dulcimer" was the creature of "a vision". See *Kubla Khan: or, A Vision in a Dream.*

[12] Aspasia, a mistress of Pericles; Lais, a Greek courtesan; and Lesbia, celebrated by Catullus, were three beautiful women whose features an artist might unite in one countenance of ideal beauty.

[13] Phyllis (Daphnis) and Chloe, two infants of Greek pastoral romance, brought up by shepherds, but finally united with their wealthy parents.

whole, but only an enormous mass of fragments and details.

In fact, he sees, in objects of sense, but the hints and germs of a universe far other than ours in which the very hedge-rows are formed of the trees of knowledge and of life, and every twinkling star is brought so near us that it dilates into a world of distinguishable glory. And, similarly, he has selected from our nature all that it contains of most precious and powerful, and concentrated these qualities into some one perfect specimen of humanity. But in the former case he fails, in the latter he succeeds; and wherefore the difference? Simply, because the one departs from the original standard of beauty in the mind, while the other merely realises and embodies the universal idea of good.

The great moral peculiarity of his writings is his constant inculcation of man's capacity for a higher condition than the present. In his vision, he sees a ladder which ascends to heaven; and he never considers us as now occupying a permanent position, but as standing merely at one point in an indefinite progression. His hopes travel faster than the world: and he casts so telescopic a view over the future that he brings the distant to his feet. But he does this mighty good, that he teaches us to look for our improvement, not to the outward circumstances over which our control must always be limited and which can return to us no substantial happiness, but to those inward powers which are beyond the reach of change or chance, to the improvement of which there is no bound assigned, and which furnish us from within with ample means for our satisfaction.

If he had done nothing more than thus to oppose the philosophy of circumstances,[14] he would have fulfilled the highest duty incumbent upon man by proclaiming to his brethren that they are masters of their own destinies; and that it only depends upon themselves to be virtuous, and thereby happy. Shelley has applied all the resources of his extraordinary genius to strengthen and illuminate this truth; and we trust the day is at hand when his writings will be studied in a kindred spirit. We are restrained, not by the strength of the shackles, but by the weakness of our own will; and the very act of choosing to be free will prove that we are so.

There are others who hold a far different doctrine from Shelley's, and who would improve our condition, not by gaining

---

[14] In this series, Jeffrey and Mackintosh are examples of thinkers practising a philosophy of circumstance or expediency.

victory over outward objects and influences and making ourselves
independent of them, but by altering those circumstances and
continuing to draw our enjoyments from them: like the Indian
girls, who show their skill and gracefulness in fetters, rather than
dance in freedom without them. Such opinions were the scorn of
Shelley, and such attempts his pity: and, thank heaven, so long as
we have poets of his noble stamp and divine ordination, we shall
have among us men of strength and courage to bear testimony
against this wanton degradation.

The instruments by which Shelley advanced these high moral
objects were a magnificent imagination, a fairy-like fancy, a
powerful intellect, a delicacy and range of perfection[15] which
were scarcely ever equalled, and a faculty of expression which,
we have no hesitation in saying, has been in our day quite unri-
valled. In this last quality we would include both richness of
diction, and the talent for composing melodious and significant
verse. Exalted as were Shelley's other endowments and accom-
plishments, in these last he stands, at least, equal to the greatest
names of our poetry. His language would by some be called
obscure, though in truth he always employs those words which
will most clearly explain his meaning. But nothing can make
intelligible a class of thoughts or feelings which we never have
ourselves experienced; and herein is the real secret of the supposed darkness of his expression. His versification is infinitely
diversified, yet uniformly perfect; now clear and simple as a
matin-bird, now rolling on like a vast river, now winding and
re-echoing like a song; and all these and a thousand more varieties
adapted, as if by intuition, to the differences of design and feeling in his different poems. So that, excepting Milton, there is
nothing in the language at all comparable to the mingled strength
and sweetness, the involved and changeful harmony, of his metre.

---

[15] Maurice explains Shelley's "range of perfection" with Coleridge's dictum of the
necessity for a "co-presence of fancy with imagination" for the highest creative
achievement. (*Biographia Literaria*, i, 194). Shawcross's note on this passage (p. 270)
cites from *Table Talk* (20 April 1833) Coleridge's further explanation of his dictum:
"Genius must have talent as its complement and implement, just as, in like manner,
imagination must have fancy. In fact, the higher intellectual power can only act
through a corresponding energy of the lower."

As Maurice employed Coleridge's "torch of guidance" in distinguishing imaginative from fanciful writers (VI, 12, p. 51), so here he applies Coleridge's dictum in a
perceptive assessment of Shelley.

SKETCH IX

Sir Walter Scott[1]

There is no living name the sound of which calls up so brilliant
and various an array of recollections as that of Sir Walter Scott.
It seems an unsatisfactory and cheerless labour to pry into the
corners and get behind the scenes of a mind which we only know
as the means of delighting us by the society of hundreds of
breathing and active beings — champions and kings, peasants and
minstrels, weird beldames, fantastic spirits, and joyous and delicate damosels. Yet why should he, who has turned mankind into
rich and bright romance, be himself exempted from the fortune
to which he has subjected all the world beside: or claim to lie hid
in the shadows of Abbotsford,[2] and pace unnoticed the highways
of *auld Reekie*,[3] while century after century is unrolled before us
in his pages, and our eyes are dazzled by the pageant of highland-
ers and chevaliers, monarchs and pilgrims? We must deal with the
spell-monger beyond the circle of his power, and cope with him
on other ground than the bush-clad rocks of his lonely valleys, or
the rugged circuit of shattered monasteries, the presence-cham-
bers of palaces now desolate, or the throng of gallants whose very
tombs are dust; and that mind which has never shone upon us
but as the sun is seen through a pictured window, when lighting
and animating crowds of saints, monarchs, and warriors — must,
we fear, be looked at through that colourless glass which is needful for the critic of mind no less than for the physical experi-
mentalist.

Sir Walter Scott is the greatest of observers. He seems to be,
like the spirits, all eye and ear; but, unlike them, he has scarcely
arrived at reflection, much less at intuition. He has looked with a

---

[1] *Athenaeum* (11 March 1828). Though a poet and novelist of enormous popular
appeal, Scott (1771-1832) founded the *Quarterly Review* (1809) as a frankly Tory
organ, thus illustrating the close connection between literature and politics.

[2] Scott's castle on the Tweed, acquired in 1812 and gradually enlarged as a family seat
for the Abbotsford Scotts.

[3] Misty, smoky Edinburgh.

close and searching and, above all, with a sympathetic eye, on
everything around him, living or inactive. He has watched
through the whole of his now waning life (and may its final close
be far distant!) the looks, the tones, the lightest indications of
passion among men. He cannot be conceived as sitting for even
an hour in a stage-coach or a coffee-room without having drawn
out and measured the characters of all his companions. Every
sensitive or irritable line about the lips, every hair of the eye-
brow upraised in the grimace and frankness of foolish admiration, or drawn together into the compressed strength of thought,
every pugnacious or friendly trembling of the finger — bring him
but for five minutes within view of them and has them noted —
each of them the germ of a picture or the hint of a personage. He
is one of the few men of our generation whom we may imagine
actually going forth like Shakespeare and Ben Jonson to "take
humours";[4] and it is a shrewd and curious art in which he must
doubtless be a thorough proficient; it is one in which a treasure
of really kind and generous feeling is of more use than wealth or
rank, or even than those other prime requisites, caution and
penetration.

Seat him in the circle round the kitchen fire of a country
ale-house, one of the blithest and most fertile scenes of study for
an humble way-faring observer; and it is impossible to doubt that
Scott would speedily win his way into the merry affections of
the whole party, find out the secrets of a dozen rough-coated
breasts, and know who are the rich ones, who the brave ones,
who the beauty, and who the oracle of the hamlet. The serving-
maid would giggle while she filled his tumbler, the landlady
smooth her apron with gracious attention while he spoke to her,
the farmer open his mouth with astonishment at his knowledge
of pigs and planting, the smith shake the rafters with a roar when
some good-humoured jest had hit the dusty miller; and the most
widely celebrated mind of modern literature would become an
intimate with ploughmen, and be held in honour by chimney-cor-
ner veterans.

Or think of him benighted in some lonely cottage, how would
he praise the ale, lay down a theory of peat-cutting, give grave
advice on the roasting of potatoes, and teach some chubby-faced

---

[4]Ben Jonson's comedy *Every Man in his Humour* was performed at the Curtain Theatre in 1598, with Shakespeare in the cast.

urchin to repeat a ballad, or bawl a Jacobite paean.[5] We know no
more of Sir Walter Scott than is known of him from the Vistula
to the Ebro;[6] but such things must have been done, such *were*
done, by the author of *Waverley*.[7] The field-preaching, the mart,
the mess-room, the courts of law and, meanest and most barren
of them all, the tables of princes — he *must* have looked at each
with this same scrutinizing good-nature, and hawk-eyed friendli-
ness. He has not only gazed upon society, but been a part of it;
he has dissected it in a spirit of joyousness, and pried into its
secrets with a frank and free-hearted curiosity.

It is in the same vein that he has been a spectator of the
outward and material world. He has never either turned from it
in weariness, or seen it through a theory; but has obviously always found in the visible universe things interesting and beautiful, not as developments of any internal law, or as a lower range
of phenomena than the human, yet filled with analogies to our
own nature, but as wide and lofty, many-coloured and various
facts, inexhaustible subjects for the healthy keenness of the
senses, and feeding the mind with an endless succession of primary, uncompounded enjoyments. The mountain and the lake,
the pine-wood and the cataract, he has wandered among them
neither with misanthropic moodiness nor quietest enthusiasm;
but to make them in fancy the stage, not of vague demons or
ministering angels, but of hundreds of busy men, clothed indeed
in the dresses of all different times and countries, yet thinking
and feeling, speaking and acting like ourselves. He has noted the
hues of clouds and shapes of crags and precipices, the carvings of
pinnacles and massiness of battlements, with the earnest and
hearty simplicity of a child; and the fresh vividness of his paintings reproduces them similarly for us.

If the description of outward objects were an end and not a
means, Sir Walter Scott would be almost a perfect writer; for we
view them in his pages through a medium nearly as pure and
colourless as the water of his Scottish hills, or the air upon their
summit; and herein he is honourably distinguished from many of
his predecessors, and some of his contemporaries. He has used his
own eyes, and written from his own perceptions; and his works

[5] A song in praise of James II.

[6] From Poland to Spain: from the east to the west of Europe.

[7] The name of Scott's first novel was suggested by his acquaintance with Waverley
Abbey, and subsequent novels by "the author of Waverley" became Waverley novels.

exhibit a fidelity of detail, and a general truth, which are a delightful restorative after mere fancy pictures. The tendency of mind, which has made him look in this way at the men and things around him, has also marked with its own peculiarities his mode of contemplating the past.

For him, history is a pageant; and as the world is a finely painted scene, so are mankind a gay procession. He sees, in bygone centuries, but heaps of brilliant facts. Every individual age and climate seems present to his thoughts as made up of certain characteristics of appearance — arms, clothes and horses, festivals and buildings, the diadem of its sovereign and the doublets of its peasants. All times and lands have thus in his memory a splendid and picturesque existence; and his mind is like the glass of the Italian wizard,[8] or the cave of Shakespeare's witches,[9] across which the portraits of dynasties, and the symbols of nations and epochs, are perpetually shifting and gleaming.

The iron times of chivalry, the glittering magnificence of the East, the barbarian wildness of the Highlands, the prison of Mary, the court of Elizabeth, the revel of Villiers, all pass before his view with equal brilliancy and motion; while the prime personages are accompanied by a train of inferior attendants, made out with the same beautiful accuracy, and animated by the same spirit of life and reality, which stir and thrill their leaders. The dim expanse of ages is thus illuminated by the various array of a gallant and triumphant throng, winding on from beneath the porch of Abbotsford, through palace and wilderness, ruined minster and merry hostel, and leaving behind them a thousand glad remembrances, even when gilded spur and sparkling carcanet have faded from before us into mist.

Yet there is in all his writings the evidence of this main defect; he knows what is, but not how or why it is so. He has seen the outward but he has not connected it with that which is within. He has looked at the conduct and listened to the speech of men; but he has not understood from what kind of central source their deeds and words are drawn. He seems to have no fondness for referring things to their origin; and instead of considering men's actions as worth observation only in so much as they illustrate

---

[8] Leonardo da Vinci, a master of many branches of study, including optics, and an example of a genius. The phrase suggests "the wizard of the north" a sobriquet bestowed upon Sir Walter Scott for the magical influence of his works upon his contemporaries. Albert R. Frey, *Sobriquets and Nicknames* (1888).

[9] *Macbeth*, IV, i, for the witch who saw the future in her glass.

the essential character of the being from which they spring, he has treated them as if they had in themselves a definite and positive value, modified in the hands of the poet and the novelist by nothing but the necessity of exciting interest and giving pleasure.

It is not that he has no systematic theory of human nature, for if he had he would to an absolute certainty be in error. But he does not appear to believe that there is any human nature at all, or that man is aught more than a means to certain external results, the which when he has described, he has done his task and fulfilled his ministry. There is incomparably more freedom and truth in his picture of our species than in the books of any of the systematic speculators, Locke, for instance, or Helvétius;[10] because he has seen the inexhaustible varieties of our doings, and has exhibited them fairly and sincerely, while such writers as those to whom we allude, have assumed some one small base, and attempted to rear upon it a fabric which, restricted and low as it is, is yet infinitely too wide and lofty for the narrowness of the foundation. But *his* idea of man is meagre and wretched, compared to that of the philosophers who have contemplated the mind, instead of measuring the footsteps; who have not sought to number the hairs upon our heads but have dealt, as it were, with the very elements of our creation.

This defect shows itself very strongly in every part of his works, where he attempts to cope alone with the thoughts of any of his personages. In his dialogues, he in some degree gets over the difficulty by repartees, passion, and mimicry of the language of the time; but in soliloquies, how barren and incomplete appears to be his psychology! And compare these or even the best parts of the conversations with a scene of Shakespeare, and the difference may at once be perceived between writers, the one of whom knows nothing but phenomena, while the other, with to the full as much of individual observation, was also imbued with the largest abundance that any man ever had of universal truth. There is scarce a page of Shakespeare that does not present us with the deepest and finest moral meditations, and with a living image of those thoughts which occupy men's minds, when they reflect upon their own nature, and attempt to overleap the bounds of the present and the actual. There is rarely anything in

[10] An interesting comparison, for Locke, the founder of philosophical liberalism, and Helvétius, a French *philosophe,* are both, like Scott, authors of "literature".

Scott that pretends to this, the highest of all merit; we doubt if there are a dozen attempts at reflection in his voluminous works; and the standard of good which he exhibits, in so far as it differs from the merest worldliness, is only raised above it by something more than usual of a certain shrewd good-humour.

Exactly similar observations hold good with regard to his treatment of things inanimate. He sees, neither in the world nor in human works anything more than so much positive existence, more beautiful or more uninteresting, larger or smaller, as the case may be, but always something to be looked at solely for itself. And herein he would be perfectly right if men had no faculty except that which has beauty for its object. There is doubtless a pleasure and a good in the contemplation of those things which are in conformity with the original idea of the beautiful in our minds; but there is also a nobler good in viewing all things around us, not merely by this one faculty, but as manifestations of still higher principles, and in connection with moral and religious truth. Even as ends in themselves almost all the objects around us have their beauty; but it is as forms and symptoms of superior and invisible powers that it is most truly useful to regard them. Nor is it necessary to put forward broadly the intention of a writer on this point; but if he has the feeling and the law within himself, their influence will be seen in every line he writes; just as in speaking of a picture, we need not explain the construction of the eye or the science of optics, though it will be obvious that we could not have thought one word about the matter without possessing the faculty of sight. It is from the want of this habit of mind that Sir Walter Scott's descriptions of scenery are in general so completely separate parts of his works; they stand out from the rest of the narrative instead of being introduced casually, indicated by an occasional expression, or shown as the drapery of the thoughts.

Besides his mode of dealing with the results of his observations of men and nature, we mentioned, as connected with it, his way of regarding history; and this is certainly no less striking than the points we have just been treating of. If the narrative of past events exhibits them to us as naked facts, it does nothing; if it presents them with their immediate cause and consequences in the minds of the actors, it does much, and what few histories have done; if it displays them justly as exponents of principles and results of the great scheme for the education of mankind, it does all that it can do. The knowledge of an occurrence is of no value whatsoever in itself.

The most spirited description of it which merely lets us know the dresses of the chief personages, how this man looked, and what that man ate, and tells us whether a sovereign died on a bed or a battle-field, gives us knowledge of nothing worth knowing. The points which deserve to be examined are those which make manifest the feelings of the persons concerned, the spirit of the times, the great designs that were at work, and were spreading to embrace ages in their circuit, the peculiarities and progress of national character; in short, what the mind of the world was, and what means were operating to improve it. The events themselves are of interest only as exhibiting human motives either in the individual or the mass, and thereby opening to us some new recesses of the soul containing perhaps powers of which we were previously unconscious, like titles to wealth, or symbols of empire, discovered in some dark and long-forgotten chamber.

Yet, in reading history, it is not upon such matters as these that Sir Walter Scott has turned his attention, but to the mere external changes and salient occurrences, to triumphs or tournaments, battles or hunting matches, to whatever can be converted into a picture, or emblazoned in a show. He has not read the annals of the earth as they ought to be studied; but he would probably not be nearly so popular a writer if he had. As it is, he has filled his mind with all that is most stirring and gorgeous in the chronicles of Europe, superstitions the more impressive because forgotten, brilliant assemblages of kings, and barons, hard-fought battles, and weary pilgrimages, characters the most desperately predominating, and events the most terrible or fantastic. Of these he has made a long phantasmagoria, the most exciting and beautiful spectacle of our day; and who can wonder or complain if he, who delights mankind with so glorious a pageant, is held by almost general consent to be the greatest of modern authors.

The tendency, which we have now dwelt upon at some length, to look at humanity and nature in their outward manifestations instead of seizing them in their inward being, has decided in what class Sir Walter Scott must be placed with reference to the moral influence he exercises. He would commonly be called one of the most moral of writers; for he always speaks of religion with respect and never depraves his writings by indecency. But ethics and religion would be the least important of studies and the human mind the simplest object in the creation if nothing more than this were needful to constitute a moral writer.[11] However, it is not so. He, and he alone, is a moral author whose works have the effect of flinging men back upon themselves; of forcing them to look within for the higher principles of their existence; of teaching them that the only happiness and the only virtue are to be found by submitting themselves uniformly to the dictates of duty, and by aiming and struggling always towards a better state of being than that which ourselves or those around us have hitherto attained.

Sir Walter Scott has observed men's conduct instead of his own mind. He has presented to us a fair average of that conduct: but he knows nothing of the hidden powers which, if strenuously and generally called forth, will leave his books a transcript of the world as erroneous as they are now accurate and honest. He has, therefore, no influence whatever in making men aim at improvement. He shows us what is, and that, heaven knows, is discouraging enough; but he does not show us what we have the means of being, or he would teach us a lesson of hope, comfort, and invigoration.

> It is our will
> Which thus enchains us to permitted ill.
> We might be otherwise; we might be all
> We dream of — happy, high, majestical.
> Where is the love, beauty, and the truth we seek,
> But in our minds? And if we were not weak,
> Should we be less in deed than in desire?
>   .   .   .
>
>   Those who try may find
> How strong the chains are which our spirit bind,
> Brittle, perchance, as straw. We are assured
> Much may be conquered, much may be endured,
> Of what degrades and crushes us. We know
> That we have power over ourselves to do
> And suffer — *what,* we know not till we try;
> But something nobler than to live and die:
> So taught the kings of old philosophy.
>   .   .   .

[11] The moral mind is an imaginative mind.

And those who suffer with their suffering kind,
Yet feel this faith religion.[12]

Though, therefore, it would be an insane malignity to call him
individually an immoral writer, as he has always recognized the
distinction between right and wrong, and never knowingly inculcated evil; yet it would be folly to pretend that he produces
much moral effect upon the world, as his works do scarcely
anything towards making men wiser or better.

The most obvious ground on which to fix his claim of a strong
and beneficial influence over men is the general and good-humoured benevolence apparent in his writings. In an age of so
much affected misanthropy and real selfishness this is doubtless a
high merit, and it is one which, in the works of Sir Walter Scott,
does not carry with it the slightest symptom of pretence or even
of exaggeration. We feel at once that we are in the presence of a
man of free and open heart disposed to laugh at every man's jest,
treat every man's foibles with gentleness, and spread over the
path of life as much as possible of manly generosity. It would be
difficult not to feel, after reading his books, that peevishness and
envy are bad and foolish propensities, that earth yields better
fruits than scorn and hatred and, above all, that there is nothing
impressive in diseased melancholy — nothing sublime in assumed
misery. His mind is evidently of the very healthiest and most
genial sort that society will admit, without avenging itself by
calumny and oppression, for a superiority which reproaches its
own viciousness.

But it should be borne in recollection that, excellent in themselves as are such qualities, and unalloyed, as they probably are in
Sir Walter Scott, a very considerable share of them is perfectly
compatible with that kind of feeling which confines itself entirely within the boundaries of our personal connections; and though
it would give up the most delicate morsel to another at the same
dinner-table, would not sacrifice a farthing to do good to a kingdom or a continent. A similar character to that displayed in the
writings of Sir Walter Scott is the result, in many cases, of mere
temperament and circumstance; though we perfectly believe that
it exists in his own breast in its purest and most meritorious
avatar.[13] The benevolence that spends itself upon whatever may

[12]Inaccurately quoted from Shelley, *Julian and Maddalo* (11. 170-191).

[13]Scott regarded Buonaparte as "a third avatar" of an "emination of the evil principle" (O. E. D.).

be brought by chance within its view, is an infinitely more agreeable quality than mere selfishness, but one that is very little likely to do any more good to mankind. We see it constantly around us, exerting itself towards every particular object it happens to stumble on; and yet perfectly indifferent and cold to the greater general designs which would do good an hundred times as extensive and a thousand times as certain.

We are not sure that Sir Walter Scott's political opinions are to be explained in this way, for we well know the vast allowances that must be made for early prejudice, confirmed by subsequent connections, habits, and interests. But we confess that it does seem to us a melancholy and painful contrast, when we think of the many warm and honest sympathies expressed and embodied in the writings of this author, and then compare them with the narrow and degraded cast of his political feelings. We think of the statue with the feet of clay;[14] of the king in the Arabian tales, the half of whose body had been changed to insensible stone;[15] of the woman in Milton, so fair above, yet terminating in such monstrous foulness;[16] of all, in short, that is strangely and fearfully discordant: for nothing in fable or vision can be more so than the politics and the romance of the writer in question. He, above all other men, would be likely to fall into such an error as this; because, from his attachment to the forms of one state of society and his indifference to the spirit of all, he could hardly avoid imagining that those forms were valuable for themselves and applicable to our own times as well as to the thirteenth century, and to London as well as to Lochaber.

The crown and the coronet still seem to him the emblems of law as opposed to anarchy, though the only countries in Europe where anarchy exists are those where the government is peculiarly despotic, as in Southern Italy, Spain, Turkey, and Ireland. He still thinks of feudalism and hereditary nobility as the causes no less than the glories of the most brilliant of modern ages, though the remains of the system are even now the greatest curses to England, and the very name of hereditary wisdom has become a

---

[14]Daniel, II, 31-35.

[15]The Young King of the Black Islands (*The Arabian Nights' Entertainment* — or *The Thousand and One Nights*).

[16]*Paradise Lost,* II, 648-53: Sin, whom Satan meets at the gate of hell.

mockery and a hissing.[17] To his eyes a splendour appears to have vanished from the world, since mankind have omitted that custom now confined (except among soldiers) to kings and courtiers, the wearing arms in peace which, much more than two thousand years ago was cited by the best of historians as the most evident relic of the rudest barbarism.[18] We fear, however, that even Sir Walter Scott himself would apostasise from the ninth to the nineteenth century if a party of English borderers were making a forage and threatening to burn Abbotsford.

It is true that no people ever existed, not living under some form of government which has, of course, grown out of their character and adapted itself, in a considerable degree, to their peculiar circumstances. We are irrevocably connected with the past — the prolongation of an antiquity which reaches back from us into the dim shades of an almost immeasurable remoteness. Every nation has within itself the germs and types of those institutions which are the most likely to produce its happiness, and which can alone be in conformity with its hereditary spirit. But these institutions must needs be altered to fit them to the varying occasions and silent revolutions of society. It is thus that Solon[19] reformed the government of Athens, when he saw that it was necessary, from the increasing power of the inferior classes, to give it a more democratic character; it is thus that the Licinian rogations[20] admitted to a larger share of authority a commonalty which had become too numerous and too strong to be safely contemned; and thus it is that, in spite of the opposition even of such men as Sir Walter Scott, the wardens, who guard the cob-webbed doors of the English constitution, will be compelled to turn the rusty hinges, and draw back the rotten bolts, and to admit to the political sanctuary an equal representation of the people.

We have spoken of the mode in which he looks at men, at nature, and at history; and attempted to show how one great defect accompanies him in each. We have said something of his

[17]Unlike property, wisdom cannot be hereditary — a concept suddenly vital to Maurice's reforming contemporaries.

[18]Thucydides, b. 1, c. 5, 6. [Maurice's note]

[19]An Athenian aristocrat who chose poverty for spiritual enrichment and was thus led to minimize class differences.

[20]Licinius Stolo and Lateranus introduced the rogations in order to equalize plebeians and patricians.

claims to be considered as a moral writer; and something of his political opinions and feelings; but connected more or less with all these subjects, there is another on which we have not hitherto touched, the necessary influence, namely, of the whole class of composition for which Sir Walter Scott is distinguished: and in speaking of the great bulk of his writings, as forming a class, we include both verse and prose, for the character of his rhymed and of his unmetrical romances is essentially the same.

The great classes into which fiction may be divided are made up of those that please chiefly by the exhibition of the human mind, and those that please chiefly by the display of incident and situation. The former are the domain of the mightier teachers of mankind; the kingdom of Homer, of Cervantes, of Shakespeare, of Milton, and of Schiller — a realm allied, indeed, to this world and open to the access of men, but pure from our infirmities and far raised above the stir of our evil passions — a sphere with which the earth is connected and moves in accordance but which, like to the sun itself, only shines upon the world to be its illumination and its law. Here is the true and serene empire of man's glory and greatness; and from this sanctuary issue the eternal oracles of consolation, which tell us to how free and sublime a destiny the human soul may lift itself.

But the other class of writers, who find their resources in everything that can create an interest however transitory and vulgar, who describe scenes merely for the purpose of describing them, and heap together circumstances that shall have a value in themselves quite independently of the characters of those whom they act upon — it is the doom of such men to compound melodramas, and the prize of their high calling to produce excitement without thought; and to relieve from listlessness, without rousing to exertion. To neither of those does Sir Walter Scott exclusively belong. That he is not one of the latter order of authors, witness much of *Old Mortality* [1816], of *The Antiquary* [1816], of *The Bride of Lammermoor* [1819], and *The Heart of Mid-Lothian* [1818]; and yet, unhappily, the larger proportion of his works would seem to separate him entirely from the former; and on the whole he has ministered immensely to the diseased craving for mere amusement, so strikingly characteristic of an age in which men read as a relaxation from the nobler and more serious employments of shooting wild-fowl or adding together figures.

Literature has become the property of the crowd, before the crowd have been made fit auditors of truth; literature has consequently been divorced from truth and degraded to their level.[2][1] But, alas! that men of genius, instead of doing something to reform their age, should submit themselves to the meanest eddies of that current which they might have turned from its wanderings to flow between banks of fragrance and beauty, and sparkle over sands of gold! Therefore, when it shall fill its appointed channel, it will leave their reputations but decaying wrecks upon the barren sands it will have deserted; and float forward, in the prouder triumph, the argosies from which it may now have shrunk away.

These are some and, we think, the chief of his errors as a writer of fiction. He has given us one work of graver pretension, the latest and the largest of his writings. But he seems to have so little idea of the essential difference between history and romance; not with regard to their comparative truth but to their different purport, that it may well be pronounced the longest and most tedious of his novels. As to the question of mere fact accuracy, we believe he has not made quite so many mistakes as are commonly charged upon him. After the account of the Revolution, which is in every way contemptible, his narrative is tolerably fair and faithful. But it is not to this we look: the *Life of Napoleon*[2][2] is the history of Europe, in the most important era it has undergone since the Reformation. It is, in the first place, the biography of a man who, in the most extraordinary circumstances, established the most wonderful empire that ever existed upon earth; who, though himself no philosopher, outwitted all the speculators of his time; who, though utterly and uniformly selfish, was sometimes more beloved, and always more admired, than any of his contemporaries; who, born in Corsican obscurity, lived to enter in triumph Milan, Madrid, Berlin, Vienna, and Moscow, to play the sovereign over France, Italy, and Germany, to re-conquer Paris from its dynasty of ages, and die a captive, in the prime of existence, on a rocky islet in a distant ocean. Such was Napoleon Buonaparte in his merely personal character; but feeble as is Sir Walter Scott's portrait of the man, how wretchedly and despicably insufficient is his account of the times!

---

[2][1] A strangely conservative note in *Sketches,* but by 1850 Maurice was convinced that education must precede the emancipation of the masses.

[2][2] *The Life of Napoleon Buonaparte, Emperor of the French with a Preliminary View of the French Revolution.* By the author of *Waverley* (9 vols., 1827), who in this year identified himself as Sir Walter Scott.

The close of the eighteenth and beginning of the nineteenth century was the period appointed for one of those sudden and violent overthrows of old institutions which, whether the forms be re-established or not, must leave them tottering and inanimate, which so break the ancient supports of habit and authority that the mere expansion of the human mind will suffice finally to destroy the super-structure. They formed one of the marked epochs of the world; a going forth of the destroyer to prepare the way for a ministry of good. The relics of other centuries were stumbling-blocks and contrasts in our path, like the antique lances and rusted helmets which grate against the ploughshare of the peasant[23] and, like him, we flung them forth from the furrows which were sown with no ignoble seed, and were to produce no scanty harvest.

But what did Sir Walter Scott discover in these things? He saw nothing but an illustration of the evils of popular resistance, of the perfections of the British Constitution, of the propriety of again subduing the continent to aristocracies and despotisms; and above all, he seems never for a moment to imagine that the French Revolution was merely one of those shadows on the dial-plate of history which follows and measures, but cannot in itself influence, the great onward movement of the human mind.

Sir Walter Scott must never again write history. He not merely knows nothing of the theory of historical composition, but he feels none of the majestic and far-seeing spirit to which alone is committed the power of unrolling the records of past centuries. He may enter into the sepulchres of buried generations, he may burst the coffins, he may breathe a new life into the bones; but he cannot decipher the hieroglyphics which would tell us how they thought; much less can he so withdraw himself from the petty influences of the present as to transmit to future times a clear picture of that which it really contains of precious and permanent.

But we trust that many years may pass before he himself becomes the property of the historian; before we shall be permitted to measure the influence of his works and the stature of his intellect without incurring suspicion and calumny; before men will be allowed to say what we have said and escape the charge of envying greatness because we ourselves are little, and of underrating the genius with which we cannot sympathize. Till

[23]Virgil, *Georgics* i. 493. [Maurice's note]

time and death have secured to all men this privilege, none can
hope more sincerely than ourselves that he will continue to vary
the dull track of ordinary existence with his gay and glittering
creations; and that if he does not defy criticism by perfection, he
will at least persevere, as he always has done, to disarm it of its
sting by the unaffected sincerity and genial kindness of his
nature.

SKETCH X

Sir James Mackintosh[1]

The reputation of this writer is very disproportionate to the extent of his definite and tangible performances. He stands in general estimation among the highest names of our day for speculative science, for politics, legislation, history, and rhetoric. Yet the works which have gained for him this high character are few and small — two or three pamphlets, a score of speeches, and as many anonymous papers in the *Edinburgh Review*. The merit of these, both for ability of thought and beauty of composition, is a sufficient warrant for the nature of the source from which they came; and we only lament that so bright a water should flow forth in such scanty streams. These writings have been sufficient to convince the world that Sir James Mackintosh is one of a small and neglected class, the lovers of wisdom. But men have done him more justice than they ordinarily render to his brethren; for he is thought of, almost on all hands, not as a dreamer of dreams, a wanderer through a limbo of vanity, but as rich in all recorded knowledge and an honest and eloquent teacher. This fame has been obtained, not by the size of his writings, but the loftiness of the ground on which they are placed, that pure and philosophical elevation from which even the smallest object will project its shadow over an empire;[2] and though vigour and perseverance are necessary to attain that height, how much larger does it make the circle of vision than when, standing among the paths of common men, our eyes are strained by gazing into the distance. It is not merely by the talent displayed in his works, brilliant and power-

---

[1] *Athenaeum* (18 March 1828). Though possessed of much learning and great understanding and an M.P. (1813-32), Mackintosh (1765-1832) is here found lacking in reason and imagination. Though, like Wordsworth, he might defend the French Revolution in 1791 only to renounce that defence in 1815, his change, unlike that of Wordsworth in *The Prelude*, records no growth of mind, but seems instead a matter of expediency.

[2] If we remember right, it is said that, from one of the Swiss mountains, the traveller may see his own shadow thrown at sunrise to a distance of many leagues. [Maurice's note]

ful as it is, nor by the quantity of his information, however various and profound, that he has obtained his present celebrity; but in a great degree, by the tone of dignity and candour, which is so conspicuous a characteristic of his mind. He has less of the spirit of party than almost any *partisan* we remember.

His greatest talent is the power of acquiring knowledge from the thoughts of others. Of the politicians of our day, if not of all living Englishmen whatever, he is incomparably the most learned. His acquaintance with the history of the human mind, both in the study of its own laws, and in action, is greater than that of any contemporary writer of our country: and his intimacy with the revolutions and progress of modern Europe, both in politics and literature, is indeed perfectly marvellous. He is also the more to be trusted in his writings on these points, because he is not very exclusively wedded to any peculiar system or even science.

Many of the chroniclers or commentators of particular tracts in the wide empire of knowledge, seem to consider that their own department is the only important one, or even that their own view of it is incalculably and beyond dispute the most deserving of attention; their works thus resemble some oriental maps in which the Indian ocean is a creek of the Persian gulf, and Europe, Asia, and Africa, are paltry appendages to Arabia. Sir James Mackintosh is, in a great degree, free from this error: and we are inclined to think, that the most valuable service he has it in his power to render to the world, would be by publishing a history of philosophy from the tenth to the seventeenth century; not because he has thought the thoughts, or felt the feelings, of those ages, but because he would give us fair and candid abstracts of the books which he had studied, and would supply questions to be answered by the oracle, of which he is not himself a priest; so that men of a more catholic, and less latitudinarian spirit, might find in his pages the elements of a wisdom to which he can minister, though he cannot teach it.

He knows whatever has been produced in other men by the strong and restless workings of the principles of their nature. But he seems himself to have felt but little of such prompting. The original sincerity and goodness of his mind display themselves unconsciously in much of his writing; but they do not appear to have given him that earnest impulsion which would have made him an apostle of truth, and a reformer of mankind. He is in all things a follower of some previously recognised opinions, because he has neither the boldness which would carry him beyond the limits consecrated by habit, nor the feeling of a moral want unsatisfied, which would have urged him thus to take a wider range. But having an acute intellectual vision, and a wish to arrive at conviction, he has chosen the best of what was before him, *within* the region of precedent and authority. He has plucked the fairest produce of the domain of our ancestors from the trees that they planted, and which have been cultivated till now in their accustomed methods.

But he has not leaped the boundaries and gone forth to search for nobler plants and richer fruit, nor has he dared to touch even the tree of knowledge which flourishes within the garden. He has looked for truth among the speculations of a thousand minds, and he has found little but its outward forms. He has abstracted something here, and added something there; he has classed opinions, and brought them into comparison; and picked out this from one, and joined on that to another; now wavered to the right, now faltered to the left; and scarce rejecting or believing anything strongly, has become learned with unprofitable learning, and filled his mind with elaborate and costly furniture which chokes up its passages and darkens its windows. He has slain a hundred systems, and united their lifeless limbs into a single figure.

But the vital spirit is not his to give. It is not the living hand of Plato or Bacon, which points out to him the sanctuary; but the monuments and dead statues of philosophers block up the entrance to the Temple of Wisdom. His mind is made up of the shreds and parings of other thinkers. The body of his philosophic garment is half taken from the gown of Locke, and half from the cassock of Butler; the sleeves are torn from the robe of Leibniz, and the cape is of the ermine of Shaftesbury; and wearing the cowl of Aquinas, and shod in the sandals of Aristotle, he comes out before the world with the trumpet of Cicero at his lips, the club of Hobbes in one hand, and the mace of Bacon in the other.[3]

[3]With *Leviathan* (1651), Thomas Hobbes became the father of English materialism, influencing Leibniz, and John Locke, whose *Essay Concerning Human Understanding* (1690) adumbrated the thought of the empiricists and became a guiding light for Shaftesbury.

The medieval Thomas Aquinas preserved Aristotle's *Logic* in the Christian thought of his *Summa Totius Theologiae,* while Francis Bacon sought to replace both with his *Novum Organum* (1620), in which he posited knowledge as man's means of dominating nature.

Joseph Butler's *Analogy of Religion* (1736) defended Christianity and argued that conscience, knowing right from wrong, must guide in matters of conduct.

Having thus formed his opinions from books, without having nourished any predominant feeling or belief in his own mind — his creed is far too much a matter of subtleties and difficulties and nicely balanced system. It is all arranged and polished, and prepared against objection, and carefully compacted together like a delicate mosaic; but it is not a portion of the living substance of his mind. It is easy to perceive, to learn, to talk about a principle, and the man of the highest talent will do this best. But to know it, it must be felt. And here the man of talent is often at fault while someone without instruction or even intellectual power, may not only apprehend the truth, as if by intuition rather than by thought, but embrace and cherish it in his inmost heart and make it the spring of his whole being.

Sir James Mackintosh has, unfortunately, buried the seeds of this kind of wisdom under heaps of learned research and difficult casuistry. He has given no way to the free expansion of his nature; nor rendered himself up to be the minister and organ of good, which will needs speak boldly wherever there are lips willing to interpret it. This, perhaps, is not seen clearly by the world. But the want is felt; and the most disciplined metaphysician, be the strength and width of his comprehension what it may, will inevitably find that men can reap no comfort nor hope in doubts and speculations, however ingenious or however brilliant, unless they hear a diviner power breathing in the voices of their teachers.

The understanding can speak only to the understanding.[4] The memory can enrich only the memory. But there is that within us of which both understanding and memory are instruments; and he who addresses it can alone be certain that his words will thrill through all the borders of the world, and utter consolation to all his kind.

He seems to us to be a man of doubting and qualifying mind, who would willingly find out the best if he had courage to despise the throng, to desert their paths, and boldly go in search of it. He heads the crowd in the road they are travelling; but he will not seek to lead them in a new direction. Nor is it only in any one particular department of thought that he seeks to support himself by the doctrines of his predecessors, and the prejudices of his contemporaries; in short, to move the future by the rotten lever of the past. It is a propensity which guides and governs him

[4]See above, VII, 3, and X, 1.

in all his labours.

In politics, he is a professed Whig; that is a man who, provided no great and startling improvements are attempted, is perfectly willing that mankind, as they creep onward, should fling off grain by grain the load with which they now are burthened: though he holds it certain that we are doomed by nature to sweat and groan for ever under by far the larger portion of our present fardels. He will not venture to conclude that the whole of a political system is bad; but his reason and his good feelings tell him that the separate parts are all indefensible. He halts perpetually between two opinions; and while decidedly a friend to the people, he is not near so certainly an enemy to bad government. He is too wise and too virtuous not to know that reform must begin; but he is too cautious and timid to pronounce how far it shall be allowed to go. What he would do in politics is all good; but he seems afraid to proceed to extremity, even in improvement.

This propensity arises in part from his natural hesitation and weakness of temperament: but is strengthened and, in his view, sanctioned by the effects of his historical studies. For he seems to have been very much influenced by the feeling of exclusive respect for the past, which is so apt to creep unconsciously and gradually, like the rust of time upon a coin, over the minds of those who devote themselves chiefly to by-gone ages. They do not see how far the path is open before us, because their eyes are constantly turned backwards; and from the same cause they are liable, in moving onward, to stumble over the slightest impediment. Sir James Mackintosh has obviously escaped (thanks to his speculative and benevolent habit of feeling) from the worst degree of this tendency; and in charging him with it at all, we are not sure that his attempt to reform the criminal law might not be held up to us as a sufficient and complete answer.

But it certainly does seem that it has acted upon him in a certain degree, in connection with the bent of his moral and metaphysical opinions, to prevent him from hoping, and therefore from attempting, any great amelioration of mankind. He is, moreover, from his habits of research and study, far too much of the professor to be all that he ought to be of the statesman. With his eloquence, his knowledge of the laws, his station in general opinion, and his seat in Parliament, he might make himself an instrument of the widest good. But alas! he retreats from the senate to the library and, when he casually emerges into affairs he, who might be the guiding star of his country, if he be not a mere partisan, appears as little better than a book-worm.

It is truly wonderful to consider, recognised by all as are the talents and acquirements of Sir James Mackintosh, how little effect he produces upon the public mind. Everybody is willing to respect his judgment and to learn from his knowledge; but the prophet will not speak. He holds a sceptre which he will not wield, and is gifted with a futile supremacy. He is one of the many able men who do nothing because they cannot do all. He seems to spend his time in storing up information for the "moth and rust to corrupt". He has none of the eager earnestness of mind, which would make him impatient at seeing the great and mingling currents of human life flow past him, without himself plunging into the stream.

He forgets that if he had written ten times as much, it would probably be only a few degrees less precious than what he has accomplished: and the world would have been influenced nearly ten times more by his abilities and knowledge. He would, doubtless, then have been prevented from heaping into his memory so much of the deeds and sayings of other men; but he would have done more good and said more truth, himself. He would not so thoroughly have known past history; but he would have been a nobler subject for future historians. Even his opinions on the constitution and laws of the human mind, he has never put forth boldly and formally; nor would it be easy to prove, from either his avowed or his anonymous productions, at what point he stands between Kant and Hume.[5]

On one great subject, namely, the essential difference between right and wrong, he has more than once declared himself; and as this point is at present of great interest and larger masses of belief seem daily ranging themselves on opposite sides, it is one with regard to which we will venture to say a very few words. It is the theory of Sir James Mackintosh that expediency is the foundation of morality, but a large and universal expediency which embodies itself in rules that admit of no question or compromise. He thus stands among the advocates of *utility,* but on the border nearest to their antagonists. His principle is obviously much less liable to fluctuation and uncertainty than that of the reasoners who, like him, basing their system on expediency, perpetually recur to the first principle of the doctrine, and will never take for

[5]Between *The Critique of Pure Reason* and a *Treatise of Human Nature,* — that is, between creative reason and fanciful association of sense data.

granted, however general may be the assent of mankind, that any rule of conduct is right unless they can demonstrate its beneficial consequence. The whole question, however, is evidently one of fact, and it would be futile to say that a different notion from that of the *Utilitarians*[6] would be more useful than theirs, supposing that, as they pretend, their creed can be proved to be the true one.

But on this ground we are content to place the matter, and we are just as certain as of the existence of our senses, that there is in the human mind a simple and primary idea of the distinction between right and wrong, not produced by experience, but developing itself in proportion to the growth of the mind. We do not say that the contrary belief is false, because it produces the state of moral disease which, we think, we can observe in the greater number of its supporters; but we maintain that it is at once the result and the evidence, in short, the symptom of that unhealthy condition. It is one of the characteristics of that mental habit in which there is so much of narrowness both in thought and feeling, and which has so strong a tendency to repress all that there is within us of nobler and more hopeful power. It seems certain that the habitual recurrence to expediency, as the standard of our conduct, must have the tendency to make us less and less moral, and more and more selfish beings; until it has completely extinguished those sympathies which unite us to all our race, and which never were acted upon uniformly by anyone who was accustomed to calculate their reaction upon himself.

That Sir James Mackintosh holds the theory of expediency in such a manner as to diminish his benevolence, we certainly do not believe. Like all the good men who have adopted this system, he probably feels a power which his intellect denies; and it is this which adds all the sanction and glory, which he and they are conscious of, to the relations that connect them with their species. But that his denial of any other basis of moral distinction than expediency has tended very much to cramp the general strain of his speculations we are just as certain; and we think that the traces of this result, or rather of the character of mind which produced both evils, may be observed in his earliest production.

---

[6] Followers of the ethical system of Jeremy Bentham (1748-1832), who adopted the creed that "the greatest happiness of the greatest number" is the guide to action. See J. S. Mill, *Utilitarianism* (1861) and D. H. Hodgson, *Consequences of Utilitarianism* (1967).

The *Vindiciae Gallicae* [1791] is a very clever book to have been written by a very young man. There is in it a completeness and vigour of reasoning, and a fullness and almost eloquence of style, which would do credit to any time of life, and justly brought distinction[7] to the youth of Sir James Mackintosh. But there is perhaps in that very nearness to excellence an evidence that there could be no closer approach. A child of three feet high, and of the exact proportions of a man, is a miracle in boyhood; but he will never grow, and the man will be a dwarf.

The mind exhibited in the work in question is not in the immaturity of greatness, but second-rate power in its highest development. There are in it none of the eager rushings to a truth, which is yet beyond our reach — none of those unsuccessful graspings at wide principles, and abortive exertions to make manifest those ideas of which as yet we only feel the first stirrings — none of those defeated attempts, the best warrant of future success which we find in the earlier works of master intellects. It is not that he has an imperfect view of an extensive field, but that he seems circumscribed by a boundary, within which all is clear to him, but beyond which he does not attempt to look. There are no chasms, such as in thinking over a subject almost every young man must have felt that he did not know how to fill up but which he knew, at the same time, required to be closed by some idea which he could not at the time command. There is nothing of this sort from beginning to end of the book; and therefore a philosopher might have predicted even then that the writer would never reform a science, or create a system.

The department of thought in which, from the time he is understood to have given to it, and from its own exceeding imperfection, he would have been most likely to work out some great regeneration, is the philosophy of international law. Yet it stands very nearly where it did: and Sir James Mackintosh does not seem even to have attempted to introduce new principles, into a mass of rule and custom that is still, in a great degree, what it was made by the necessities or ignorance of our semi-barbarous forefathers. He seems to us, in short, to be distinguished chiefly by readiness in accumulating the thoughts of others, by subtlety in discerning differences, and by the greatest power of expression which can exist without anything of poetical imagination.

[7] A defence of the French Revolution as an answer — which Mackintosh later repudiated — to Burke's *Reflections on the French Revolution* (1790).

SKETCH XI

Maria Edgeworth[1]

We should incur the contempt of Miss Edgeworth, if we were to affect to treat her with any peculiar forbearance on account of her sex. The character of our previous speculations on the authors of our day is, we trust, a sufficient warrant to our readers that we shall not indulge in scurrility or wilful misrepresentation; and within this limit, to which we confine ourselves, not for her sake, but for our own, there is no freedom of discussion which the lady, whose name we have just set down, would not herself grant to us. She would do so on principle.

But she has nothing to fear in so doing. For no one, who is capable of understanding her works, could feel even a moment's temptation to visit her with the slightest disrespect. Her talents would ensure to her a high degree of admiration, if any talents could in themselves be admirable; but her evident wish to do good, however men may differ in judgment as to her success, *must* always obtain esteem. Independently in a great degree of these merits, she has secured to herself another ground of favourable consideration. For a large and active portion of the instructed society of England connect her name with the remembrance of much early enjoyment.

We know not any mode whereby the friendly sympathy of so many persons may be won, as by writing agreeable books for children. In an age which is not so often happy as in later life, we are commonly willing to persuade ourselves, such books as *Harry and Lucy* [1825], and the *Parent's Assistant,*[2] supply a keen and enduring pleasure; and we look back to them with the more

---

[1] *Athenaeum* (28 March 1828). Influenced by the Coleridgean distinction between reason and understanding, Maurice saw and condemned a Benthamite principle in the work of Maria Edgeworth (1767-1849). *Practical Education,* a joint work of Miss Edgeworth and her father, appeared in 1798, the year of *Lyrical Ballads,* whose authors, by contrast, aimed to educate society by re-awakening the natural feelings.

[2] Stories for children, the first part appearing in 1796, but published in six volumes in 1800.

delight, because there are seldom many points in our childhood to which we can thus recur. He, in whose infant hands these little volumes have been placed, associates them through all the turbulence or dullness of his after days with the brook, the bridge, the ruined castle, the hay-field, the orchard, and the bank of primroses, which supplied to these tales, no less than to his own existence, a beautiful and heart-felt scenery. That "wisdom" of feeling, which "sits with children round its knees", would prevent us from speaking harshly of Miss Edgeworth, if we were for an instant so inclined, and would hold up the smiles of infancy to turn aside the deadlier weapons of criticism.

This lady has been tolerably miscellaneous in the forms of her writings, but not so in the substance. Letters, essays, dramas, narratives all seem written on one plan, and intended for one single purpose. Her novels are the most celebrated, the most voluminous and, perhaps, the best of her works. They have somewhat declined in celebrity but they must always have a certain value as pictures in the Irish national gallery; and their present comparative obscuration arises, not from any difference of opinion on this point, but from the riotous popularity of the more varied, animated, and picturesque productions which our age has so profusely multiplied.

Miss Edgeworth, or rather her system, has little chance of any brilliant success in a contest of this kind. For though few of the writers of fiction in our time and country have a clear or adequate idea of the laws and object of art, many of them feel that it has rules and purposes of its own, which make it an end in itself, and not a mere accessary or instrument of some other design. Miss Edgeworth always has some one definite moral aim; and we read her works, not as specimens of ideal creation, but as lectures on matters of social convenience. She wishes to instruct and improve the world and, with this view, she has written tales for children of various ages, for persons of the more ignorant classes, and for ladies and gentlemen.

Of all the personages whom she brings upon the stage in these narratives the most real and lively are the Irish poor. The three great describers of the lower orders of Irishmen are Miss Edgeworth, Lady Morgan,[3] and the author of the *Nowlans*.[4] The

[3]Lady Morgan née Sydney Owenson (1783-1859) made her reputation as a writer of Irish romances.

[4]John Banim (1798-1842) wrote *Tales of the O'Hara Family*, the second series of which comprised *The Nowlans* and *Peter of the Castle* (3 vols., 1826). See Andrew Block, *The English Novel 1740-1850 A Catalogue*, with an introduction by John Crow and Ernest A. Barker (1961).

portraits of the last-named author, perhaps, in some degree exaggerated the energy, and those of Lady Morgan, the oddity of their countrymen.

The fault of Miss Edgeworth is of another kind. Her figures are too much detached and filed to fit the niche. They are framed and glazed, or dried and pressed, like specimens in a *hortus siccus*.[5] There is evidently much about these descriptions which results from long and accurate observation. But there is also something which comes from the resolution to embody an abstract idea. She has philosophised upon irregularity till she has made it almost systematic. The potato is served, not only with the coat off (itself an abomination to all true Milesians), but after having been subjected to some process of French cookery.

Yet we thank her for this part of her works. She was the first writer who gave us an idea of an Irishman as aught else than a compound of thick legs and bold blunders; and cried down the brass money which had so long been passing in foreign countries for the genuine national coin. Herein she rendered a great service; for the Irishman is not only an admirable addition to our list of personages, but a being whom it especially behoves us to study and to understand. To comprehend him thoroughly, to know with how many splendid gifts the varied influence of natural circumstances supplied him, and to how deep a criminality he has been driven by that British Constitution which stepped in, like the malignant fairy in the fable, to render all those gifts of no avail — to acquire this knowledge, it will not be sufficient to read Miss Edgeworth. But she will undoubtedly give large assistance provided we remember always, that her own philosophy is completely one of calculation and that she is not, therefore, the best judge of a being of impulse, any more than a painter whose eye has been entirely educated for form can be trusted in delineating colour.

But it is not the same with regard to her gentlemen and ladies. In most of her portraits of this kind, nothing is valuable but the system which they embody. She makes the elements and essence of her personages consist of certain principles of morals and, in the attempt to invest them with life and individuality, she exaggerates some accidental differences, makes them stiff with elaborate ease and, while she endeavours to keep them in perpetual motion, breaks the very spring which impels the automatons. As

[5] A collection of dried plants.

her single figures are not "portraits", nor any of her novels that ideal whole which we commonly call an "historical picture", we can only consider them as manifestations of a system; and to this system we must direct our attention.

The main tendency of her opinions is to exalt the understanding over the feelings, and to direct it to the one object of procuring happiness for the individual. Herein she seems to us to be wrong. If we cultivate the understanding and make it the guide and master of the feelings, their natural goodness will be entirely stifled or perverted; and it is only in the full development of these that happiness and virtue are to be found. But if we cherish, in the first place, all the better impulses, and let them govern both the understanding[6] and the reason, as their instruments, the intellectual powers will be called forth just as strongly as if their perfection were the final object of desire and, instead of being limited to our personal sphere, will be taught to expand more widely and to embrace the vast domain of the universe, to every portion of which the free sympathies of man will more nearly or more distantly unite him.

But Miss Edgeworth is unhappily but one of that large class of ethical writers who maintain that we must look solely to the improvement of the thinking faculties of men for any chance of ameliorating their condition: — that there is one simple, undeniable principle — the wish for our own enjoyment — which forms the foundation of all ethics: — that we must consider the right regulation of this principle as the only means of producing moral good: — and that, if we could elevate mankind to the condition of pure intelligences, we should have done all that is possible for securing human happiness. Among these persons, several French· and some English writers are especially conspicuous; but by far the most remarkable *body* of them flourished in France during

---

[6]It is one of the great peculiarities of Mr. Coleridge's philosophical writings, that they uniformly dwell upon the distinction between these faculties, as being laid in the foundations of the human mind. He has, unfortunately, been far less listened to than he deserves. A late article, in the *Edinburgh Review* on German Literature ["The State of German Literature", *Edinburgh Review*, XLVI (October 1827), 304-51], supports this same belief, but puts it forward as if it were to be found only in German writers, and were utterly unknown in our native metaphysics. The author of the paper in question, though an able and instructed writer and animated by an excellent spirit, is yet evidently ignorant of the works of Coleridge and has therefore, in some instances, gone abroad for truths which he might have found at home. Perhaps, however, we ought to conclude, from the past conduct of the rulers of the *Edinburgh Review*, that they would not have admitted any praise of the first of living philosophers. [Maurice's note]

the last century.[7] These were men, not indeed of much eloquence, not of profound meditation, or very extensive views —
but persons of exceeding acuteness, of inimitable talent for
subtle ridicule and grave satire, of keen observation for detecting
the lurking basenesses of motive and character — of more fancy
than feeling, and more wit than wisdom. It would not be difficult
to show to what extent this system prevailed in the ancient
Greek philosophy, or to trace it in English writers previous to
Miss Edgeworth. We shall not now attempt this; but we would
remark that the doctrine contains one point particularly calling
for observation.

The great assumption which stands as the corner-stone of this
theory, is the statement that every human being acts from the
one *sole* motive of a regard to his own enjoyment. The degree to
which this belief has haunted the literature of France is a singular
phenomenon; and we find it broadly laid down in the *Thoughts*
of a man of a far higher stamp and nobler school than the succeeding philosophers of his country, the unhappy but illustrious
Pascal.[8] He tells us:

> All men, without a single exception, desire to be
> happy. However various may be the methods they
> employ, this is the end at which they all aim. It is
> this same desire, accompanied in each by differ-
> ent views, which makes one man join the army,
> and another stay at home. *The will never takes
> the slightest step but towards this object. This is
> the motive of every action of every man,* even of
> him who hangs himself.[9]

The supporters of this doctrine will tell us, be it remembered,
that, by the enjoyment which they maintain to be the object of

[7]The *Philosophes* and *L'Encyclopédie (see above, I, 2 and II, 6).*

[8]The author of *Pensées* (1670).

[9]Maurice's note, inaccurately cited and quoted from *Pensées de Pascal,* edited by
Ernest Havet (Paris, 1885), p. 145, Article VIII:
  Tous les hommes desirent d'être heureux: cela est sans exception. Quelque
  differens moyens qu'ils y employent, ils tendent tous à ce but. Ce qui fait que
  l'un va à la guerre, et que l'autre n'y va pas, c'est ce même désir qui est dans
  tous les deux, accompagné de differentes vues. La volonté ne fait jamais la
  moindre démarche que vers cet objet. C'est le motif de toutes les actions de
  tous les hommes, jusqu'a ceux qui se tuent et qui se pendant. *Pensées de
  Pascal,* xxi, 1.

all human actions, they do not mean the kind of gratification sought for by what is *commonly* called self-interest. They include the pleasures of sympathy in their list of motives; and their proposition therefore amounts to this, that the desire which prompts us to commit every action of our lives, is a desire to procure for ourselves enjoyment of some kind or other, and that the motive of what would commonly be called the most generous exertion, is a wish for the satisfaction to be obtained by ourselves from the success of that exertion, or from the complacency with which we regard the exertion itself.

Now this is not a dogma, the truth or falsehood of which is to be shown by any reference to history. We may search all the records of past experience to establish a fact which our consciousness is sufficient to demonstrate; namely, that the highest enjoyment does arise from the performance of generous actions; but we shall not then have approached at all nearer to a solution of the difficulty unless we can also show that the aim which governed the mind, previously to the performance of such actions — that the object to procure which they were performed — was the pleasure that we know must have followed them: — unless it can be proved that the gratification of the individual, as it was to be the consequence, must, therefore, have been the cause of the conduct.

Here is the matter at issue between the sects; and the advocates of the system in question must immediately be worsted unless they can venture to affirm that no wish is ever present to the mind, previous to the performance of any action, except the desire for our own enjoyment. On this subject there is no judge but our own experience — no oracle but in our bosoms; to this arbiter we must refer for an answer, and before this tribunal we may safely challenge our opponents. The natural infirmities of the mind, degrading systems of education, corrupt forms of government, sophistical codes of morality, and the tyrannous laws of a public opinion, which these things, together with partial, though despotic, interests, and an ignorance consecrated by ages, have united to pollute and pervert — all these have exercised an almost unrestrained dominion over every human being. There is no one living who has not ample cause to blush at the recollection and weep over the effects of habitual and almost unnoticed immoralities — if not to feel a remorse, which most of us are doomed to experience, for errors of a deeper dye. Yet there is not, we may trust, a single individual of our species who cannot

draw consolation from remembering at least one moment of unmingled virtue in which, without shrinking from personal danger
and without a thought of personal enjoyment, his voice has been
uplifted to warn, or his hand outstretched to save.

We may not have rescued a life by perilling our own: we may
not have exalted a nation from wretchedness, by presenting ourselves as victims to the swift vengeance of the dungeon and the
scaffold, or to the more agonizing martyrdom of long and universal obloquy; we may not have sacrificed our dearest and most
intimate affections in the cause of truth, and charity, and religion: — but who is there that cannot cheer his hours of sorrow or
calm the fierceness of inquietude by recalling some unostenta-
tious impulse of love, some humble deed of self-denial, which has
gushed pure from the fresh fountains and deep recesses of the
spirit, undarkened by a tinge of that feeling which aims but at
our own pleasure? Such sensations are the most consoling enjoyments, such recollections are the holiest relics, which our existence affords; but make the prospect of this delight the object of
our exertions, and it will fly from the grasp that seeks it. It is a
shadow which follows the journeyings, and will assuredly bless
the aspirations, of virtue; but it forever eludes our embrace when
we turn back from the appointed path to pursue its footsteps.

It has been wisely ordained that on the purity of the motive
shall depend the sweetness of the reward — that, if we calculate
the amount of the hire, the worthless task will have been performed in vain. We can never hope to participate in this noblest
gratification, this solemn harmony of the soul, but by cherishing
that inward glory and immortal fire which, like the coal from the
altar, has power to purify our lips and, like the blazing column,
will guide our footsteps through the wilderness. And for those in
whose breasts it has been choked and stifled, to them we cannot
prove the existence of feelings on which they have habitually
trampled. These men have thrown away that which is of greater
price than members, or organs, or senses; and the boldness of
their unbelief is a guarantee for nothing but the misery and debasement of their condition.

But it may be replied, you merely delude yourselves with a
dream of unnatural sentiment. You arrive, by habit, at hiding
from your own apprehensions the feelings under which you act;
and· the calculation, whether any benevolent action which you
contemplate will procure enjoyment, is at length performed so
rapidly that you overlook the steps of the process. Such is a

common and a bold assertion, the refutation of which is simply this: — we have no evidence as to the state of our minds, under any circumstances, except from consciousness; and there are innumerable cases in which we are conscious of no such process as that supposed, but are conscious of sensations directly opposed to, and utterly incompatible with it.

Again, it will be asserted, the desire of performing a beneficent action is a want analogous to hunger and the gratification of it is attended with pleasure as is the satisfying our appetites with food. But the obvious and direct tendency of appeasing the cravings of hunger is to give pleasure to no one but ourselves; the plain and immediate effect of this supposed moral want is to give enjoyment to others; and when the cases differ in so material a circumstance, it is an impudent assumption of the whole matter in dispute to infer that they are similar in other respects. Here, as before, it is merely assertion against assertion.

But the statement of the disciples of Epicurus and Bentham is sometimes, we may trust, rendered worthless even by their own conduct; and there are men that maintain this theory who, if a case occurred that required their exertions, would undoubtedly rush forward without a moment's reference to self, in the might of that glorious impulse which they deny in words, but which would best be demonstrated by the overpowering voices of their own bosoms.

Even allowing that the greater part of men are conscious of no such feelings — an opinion which the hearts of the most ignorant and debased of our kind are powerful to refute — even allowing this, yet are there recorded spirits of a loftier nature and deeds of a purer beneficence with which we never can sympathise, but by lifting our minds to the conception of emotions far different from those imputed to the whole species. When we picture the Swiss patriot who hurled himself on the spears of Burgundy[10] for the salvation of his country, it is possible to imagine that, during those moments of brief and burning excitement, any sentiment can have throbbed in his breast but the passion to redeem a people from instant and overwhelming tyranny?

Or stand in the dungeon of the martyr, and he will be seen

[10] See Scott, *The Battle of Sempach* (1818), a literal translation of an ancient Swiss ballad of Tchudi, the cobbler and minstrel, upon the battle, fought 9 July 1386, being the victory by which the Swiss cantons established their independence and in which Arnold von Winkelried (a real person) is said to have performed his legendary feat of arms.

looking through its shadows to the prospect of a futurity that shall exalt the destinies of mankind; not coiling his soul into its own recesses to meditate on the reward of his sufferings, but with hopes that embrace all time and all existence, and with a brow that throbs, and an eye that gleams, under the vision of generations yet to come, who will find in his memory the prolific seeds of human amelioration, and will kindle a torch to enlighten the world, at the eternal flame which burns in the tomb of the persecuted philosopher.

It seems to many minds the most certain of all the phenomena in the science of moral philosophy — it is one of the truths of which we have not the slightest doubt — that the enjoyment which we are intended to derive from the practice of virtue is entirely dependent on the motive under which we act. Thus far we may agree with our opponents — that it is the duty of every man to build up his own mind into the greatest perfection of which it is susceptible. But as to the character in which that perfection consists, we should differ on every point. That perfection is dependent far more on the moral excellence than on the intellectual power of the mind, inasmuch as he is more likely to arrive at his object who pursues the right path at however great a distance, than he who, apparently far nearer and journeying more rapidly, yet moves in a wrong direction. The object of the purest and noblest ambition must ever be, in despite of passion and of interest, to rear from that holy germ which is planted in the heart of every man the healing and immortal herb, the *moly*[11] of a purer deity than Hermes, and of a wiser than Pallas, which alone can strengthen us against temptation, and alone can soothe us in sorrow; than which no other can enable us to be uniformly ministers to the happiness of others, and thereby to secure our own.

It was in cherishing these seeds of love and feeding them with the sustenance of lofty thoughts — it was in this labour that Plato lived his life, and Socrates encountered death; it was this endeavour which enlightened the blindness and consecrated the studies of Milton; it is this high exertion which has poured over the pages of Leighton[12] and of Pestalozzi[13] its flood of tenderness and

[11] A herb, endowed with magic properties, which Hermes gave Odysseus to protect him from the charms of Circe (*Odyssey*, Bk. X).

[12] Robert Leighton (1611-84), an advocate of toleration, whose simple and dignified prose was, in Coleridge's view, inspired.

[13] J. H. Pestalozzi (1746-1827), a Swiss educational reformer, who loved children.

beauty; it is to such glorious attempts, neglected as they are by self-styled philosophers for the miserable triumphs of vanity and the degrading struggles of avarice and sensuality; it is to such attempts that we must look for all real improvement of our kind: for the principle of the soul's perfection is universal love — the principle which has made the martyrs, the heroes, the poets, and the philosophers of the world, the strength of the humble, the only consolation of the broken spirit.

The most important influence of philosophical belief is that which it exerts on the education of the young. To this purpose Miss Edgeworth has directed her opinions, and exactly in proportion as her moral system is false are her schemes of education erroneous. We do not say that it is not an object with her to make men self-denying, benevolent, brave, and true; but that the main end which she proposes to herself is to produce the habit of governing the mind by calculation and self-interest. The basis of her plan is the general principle that we should associate pleasure with whatever we wish that our pupils should pursue, and pain with whatever we wish that they should avoid.

Now, this practice will infallibly tend to consecrate in the eyes of children, the belief that they ought to make their own enjoyment the object of their actions; and, to say nothing of the impossibility of any man uniformly calculating rightly, the custom of constantly regarding the result of our actions to ourselves, produces a selfish state of mind, which necessarily brings with it discontent and misery. Moreover, if we make the motive of conduct to be the prospect of the consequences, which we have experienced to follow certain actions, those consequences having sprung from the arrangement and will of the persons around us, we shall speedily learn when we get beyond the domain of these prepared influences that the same discipline and government are no longer at work, and we shall cease to let our past experience control us when we know that we are released from any similar operation for the future.

It may undoubtedly be said in defence of Miss Edgeworth's principle, though not of her application of it that, by the ordination of God and the nature of man, suffering is consequent upon evil doing and that enjoyment waits upon the footsteps of virtue. But this is not the suffering or the enjoyment wherewith Miss Edgeworth would pay or punish. *This* system is one which, being founded in the first principles of humanity, must always be independent of times and circumstances; but it is one of the gravest defects of the plan we are considering that it almost entirely omits to make use of the means supplied to us by the Creator.

Miss Edgeworth founds none of her processes upon the feeling of the difference between right and wrong, upon the innate tendency to benevolence, or upon the idea of the Divine Nature of which the seed is sown within us. When the foundation of rock is ready for the hands of the mason, she prefers to build upon the sand; and with all that is most permanent and precious, the very essential elements of the universe given to us as the grounds and materials of education, she would betake herself to a shadow and a sound. But the object she would attain cannot thus be reached; nor is it possible to sustain a superstructure of granite on a base of vapour. If the two kinds of improvement were inconsistent, the world could better be without the inventions of art and the discoveries of science, without steam-engines and political economy, than it could want earnestness and goodness, kindly affections, generosity, piety, and truth. But thanks be to heaven! there is no such inconsistency; and the more freely and completely our best feelings are developed, the stronger will be our motives for pursuing every inquiry and undergoing every labour which can tend to the advantage of mankind.

SKETCH XII

Lord Byron[1]

The mind of a poet of the highest order is the most perfect mind that can belong to man. There is no intellectual power and no state of feeling which may not be the instrument of poetry, and in proportion as reason, reflection or sympathy is wanting, in the same degree is the poet restricted in his mastery over the resources of his art. The poet is the great interpreter of nature's mysteries, not by narrowing them into the grasp of the under-standing, but by connecting each of them with the feeling which changes doubt to faith. His most gorgeous and varied painting is not displayed as an idle phantasmagoria, but there flows through all its scenes the clear and shining water which, as we wander for delight or rest for contemplation, perpetually reflects to us an image of our own being. He sympathises with all phenomena by his intuition of all principles; and his mind is a mirror which catches and images the whole scheme and working of the world. He comprehends all feelings, though he only cherishes the best; and even while he exhibits to us the frenzies or degradations of humanity, we are conscious of an ever-present divinity, elevating and hallowing the evil that surrounds it.

A great poet may be of any time, or rank, or country; a beggar, an outcast, a slave, or even a courtier. The external limits of his social relations may be narrow and wretched as they will, but they will always have an inward universality. In his rags, he is nature's treasurer: though he may be blind, he sees the past and the future, and though the servant of servants, he is ever at large and predominant.

But there are things which he cannot be. He cannot be a scorner, or selfish, or luxurious and sensual. He cannot be a

---

[1] *Athenaeum* (8 April 1828). George Noel Gordon (1778-1824), sixth Baron Byron, to whom, in spite of former refusals, a memorial was belatedly unveiled in Westminster Abbey on 8 May 1969. While the Dean feared that he and the Chapter might seem to be infected with modern permissiveness, yet Byron, he explained, was a poet; and Maurice would have agreed. "Into heaven, perhaps not; but into the Abbey, certain-ly." *Manchester Guardian Weekly* (15 May 1969), p. 7.

self-worshipper, for he only breathes by sympathy, and is its
organ; he cannot be untrue, for it is his high calling to interpret
those universal truths which exist on earth only in the forms of
his creation. He cannot be given up to libertine debauchery; for it
is impossible to dwell at once before the starry threshold of
Jove's court, and in the den of lewd and drunken revel. It was to
Hades, not to Olympus, that the comrades of Ulysses voyaged
from the island of Circe;[2] nor can we pass, without long and hard
purgation, from the sty to the sanctuary, or from the wine-cup to
the fountain of immortality.

The poet must be of a fearless honesty; for he has to do battle
with men for that which men most dread, the regeneration,
namely, of man: and yet he must be also of a loving-kindness; for
his arms are the gentleness of his accents, and the music of all
sweet thoughts. Such is the real and perfect poet; and it is only in
so far as verse-artisans approach to this that they are entitled to
that lofty and holy name. But he who is such as has been now
described, is indeed of as high and sacred a function as can belong to man. It is not the black garment, nor the precise and
empty phrase which makes men ministers of God; but the communion with that Spirit of God, which was in all its fullness upon
those mighty poets, Isaiah and Ezekiel;[3] which unrolled its visions over the rocks of Patmos,[4] and is, in larger or smaller
measure, the teacher of every bard.

Many of the warmest admirers of poetry will of course be
shocked at the idea of its being anything more than an innocent
amusement. It is in their eyes a pretty pastime to be classed with
the making of handscreens or the shooting of partridges, an art
not at all more important and only a little more agreeable, than
rope-dancing or backgammon, to be resorted to when we are
weary of the graver and more difficult operations of summing up
figures or filling sheepskins with legal formulas. These are the
persons who are perfectly contented with a poet if he supplies
them with excitement at the least possible expense of thought;
who profess that the *Faerie Queene* is tedious and uninteresting,

---

[2] As the comrades of Ulysses failed to struggle against Circe and were changed into
swine, so without effort men sink into the lower world instead of rising to Mount
Olympus, the fabled home of the Greek gods.

[3] Prophets are poets and poets, prophets.

[4] The island in the Aegean Sea where, according to legend, St. John saw the vision of
the Apocalypse.

who only do not despise Milton because he is commonly re-
ported to have been a man of genius, who treat Wordsworth as a
driveller and Coleridge as a dreamer of dreams. And herein they
are, perhaps, right; for, being deaf, they have not heard the pip-
ing, and how then could they dance? We trust, however, that we
have many readers who will agree with us in taking a different
view of these matters, and to them we would say a few words
about Lord Byron.

No one, probably, will be inclined to maintain that Lord
Byron's poetry produces a good moral effect, except those who
are anxious to spread the disbelief of the goodness of God, and
to bring about the promiscuous intercourse of the sexes. With
such persons we have at present no quarrel. They are welcome to
their opinions so far as we are concerned; and we can only lament, for their own sakes, that they should think and feel as they
do.

To those who, without going so far as these, yet deny that his
writings have a bad moral influence, we will give up the advantage to be derived from pressing the two above-mentioned points,
and put the question on other grounds: and we wish to state
distinctly that we think, in the first place, Lord Byron (as seen in
his writings) had no sympathy with human nature and no belief
in its goodness; and, secondly, that he had no love of truth.[5]
These are grave charges; and, at least, as grave in our eyes as in
those of any of our readers. But we are convinced of the justice
of them; and no fear of being classed with the bigots, of being
called churchmen rather than Christians and believers in articles
more than believers in God, shall prevent us from expressing and
enforcing our conviction.

The attempt to prove anything as to the habitual state of mind
of a writer, by picking out detached sentences from his works,
we look upon as vain and sophistical; vain, because no sentence
of any author expresses the same meaning when detached from
the context as when taken along with it; sophistical, because the
very selection and abruption of these parts indicates a wish to
persuade us that we ought to judge of a house from a single
brick. The only satisfactory and honest method of estimating an
author is by considering the general impression which his works
leave upon the mind.

Now, if any candid and reflecting man (or woman) were to

[5] Byron is not a poet in the highest sense of that word.

inform us of the influence exerted upon him by the perusal of one of Lord Byron's poems, would not his account be something of this sort — that he had felt inclined to look with scorn and bitterness upon his fellow-creatures, to wrap himself up in his own selfishness, and to see in the outward world, not embodyings of that one idea of beauty which prevails in our own minds, not frame-works for human conceptions and affections, but mere images of his own personality and vantage-grounds on which to raise himself afar from and above mankind? Would he not say that he had been imbibing discontent, disgust, satiety, and learning to look upon life as a dreary dullness, relieved only by betaking ourselves to the wildest excesses and fiercest intensity of evil impulse? If, as we firmly believe, a sincere observer of himself would give us this account of his own feelings after communing with the poetry of Byron, the question as to its beneficial or even innocent tendency is at an end.

It is true that there are in man higher powers than those which tend directly to action; and there may be a character of a very exalted kind, though not the most perfect, which would withdraw itself from the business of society, and from the task of forwarding the culture of its generation to contemplate with serene and grateful awe the perfect glory of the creation. But this is not the species of superiority to those around us and independent of them, which is fostered by the works of Lord Byron.

The feeling which runs through them is that of a self-consuming scorn and a self-exhausting weariness, as remote as can be from the healthful and majestic repose of philosophic meditation, as different from it as is the noisome glare of a theatre from that midnight firmament which folds the world in a starry atmosphere of religion; while the practical portion of our nature is displayed in his writings as only active and vigorous amid the atrocities or the vileness of the foulest passions. He saw in mankind not a being to be loved, but to be despised; and despised, not for vice, ignorance, insensibility, or selfishness, but because he is obliged, by a law of his being, to look up to some power above himself, because he is not self-created and self-existing, nor "himself, his world, and his own God".[6]

As the Lord Byron of *Childe Harold* [1812] and *Don Juan* [1818-24] had no sympathy with mankind, neither does he seem to us to have had any love of truth. He appears to have felt that

[6] Like Milton's Satan.

we have a natural tendency towards admiring and feeling in accordance with the show of bold and bad predominances. The corrupt vanity of men, the propensity[7] which teaches them to revere Cromwell and worship Napoleon, has made the world derive a diseased gratification from the pictures of Harold and Conrad. But these latter personages are essentially untrue. All that gives them more of the heroic and romantic character than the former worthies, is superadded to the original basis of evil and worthlessness, and is utterly inconsistent with it. And this, Lord Byron must have known. He who put together these monsters must have been aware that they are as false and, to a philosopher, as ridiculous, as sphynxes or chimeras to a naturalist. But he had so little love of truth that he could not resist the temptation of encircling himself with these bombastic absurdities, to raise the astonishment of sentimental mantua-makers.

It is mournful to see that so much of energy and real feeling should have been perverted to the formation of these exaggerated beings, alternately so virtuous and so vicious, now so overflowing with tenderness and so bright with purity, and again so hard, and vile, and atrocious. These qualities, to be sure, are all found in man; but the combination, where in earth or moon shall we look to find it? The principles of human nature are not mere toys like phosphorus and paint wherewith to eke out goblins: and he who pretends to exalt the mind by representing it as superior, not only to its meaner necessities, but to its best affections, in truth degrades it to the basest of uses by exhibiting it, not as a thing to be reverenced, and loved, and studied with conscientious and scrutinising reflection, but as a dead and worthless material which he may pound and compound — evaporate into a cloud or analyse into a *caput mortuum,* and subject to all the metamorphoses which are worked by the lath wand of a conjuror.

It is only by attributing the favourite thoughts and deeds of his writings to personages whom we feel throughout, though we may not realise the consciousness, to be essentially different from ourselves that he could for a moment beguile us into conceiving libertinism sublime, and malignity amiable; and if mankind were so educated as to know the constitution of their own souls, if they had learned to reflect more and to remember less, they would never be deluded into sympathy with phantoms as unsubstantial and inconsistent as the Minotaur, the Scylla, the

[7]Self-willed, ruthless determination.

Harpies, and the Cyclops of fable — the Anthropophagi, and men whose heads "Do grow beneath their shoulders".[8]

We entirely omit the question of the direct irreligion and indecency of his writings. As to these matters, those who feel religiously will blame him without our assistance, and those who approve of infidelity or gloat over obscenity will applaud in spite of us. At present, we neither seek to heighten the reprobation, nor to diminish aught from the approval. For ourselves, we lament the anti-Christian and impure tendencies of his mind, not so much for any positive evil they can do — this, we suspect, being much over-rated — as because they are evidences of the degradation of a powerful mind and of the pollution of much and strong good feeling.

We certainly differ considerably from the greater number of those who have attacked him as to the particular parts of his writings which merit the severest condemnation. The story of Haidee seems to us much less mischievous than that of Donna Julia, and this far more endurable than the amour with Catherine. *Childe Harold* will do more harm than *Cain*,[9] and either of them more than the parody of *The Vision of Judgment* [1821]. Of this also we are sure, that had he never openly outraged public opinion by direct blasphemies and grossness, the world would have been well enough content to receive his falsifications of human nature for genuine; and all his forced contortions and elaborate agonies would have passed current as natural manifestations of a reasonable and pretty despair. But, when he once did violence to those names which are the idols of the age, while the spirit of religion is wanting, he became a mark for the condemnation of those who live by the service of Bel and Dagon.[10] He might exhibit man as a wretched and contemptible, an utterly hopeless and irrecoverably erring creature,— he might represent selfishness and vanity as the true glories of our nature — he might leave us no home but solitude and no stay but sensuality, and deny not only God, but good — and yet be the favourite of pious reviewers, the drawing-room autocrat, the boudoir deity.[11] But

---

[8] *Othello*, I, iii, 144-45. Byron's characters are like minotaurs, harpies, and anthropophagi — all fabulous, but deformed monsters.

[9] *Cain: A Mystery*, a tragedy (1821).

[10] Popular idols of the fashionable world.

[11] A telling reference to the complacence of the nineteenth century.

when he once dared to doubt, in so many words, of the wisdom of Providence and, instead of hinting adultery, to name fornication, the morality of a righteous generation[12] rose up in arms against him; and those who ought long before to have wept over the prostitution of such a mind, affected a new-born horror at the event, though they had been delighting for years in the reality of the pollution.

We wish not to deny that Lord Byron was a poet, and a great one. There are moods of the mind which he has delineated with remarkable fidelity. But, as Shakespeare would not have been what he is, had he exhibited only the fantastic waywardness of Hamlet, or the passionate love of Romeo, so Byron is less than a first-rate poet for the uniformity with which he has displayed that intense self-consciousness, and desperate indifference, which he has undoubtedly embodied more completely than any other English writer.[13] The sceptre of his power is, indeed, girt with the wings of an angel, but it is also wreathed with earth-born serpents; and while we admire we must sigh, and shudder while we bow.

[12]Though complacent, and foolishly following many gods, the nation still preserves her fundamental integrity.

[13]The greatest poets reveal love for man, reverence for truth, and devotion to art.

SKETCH XIII

Mr. James Mill[1]

The reputation which this writer has achieved is the strongest evidence of the practical character of English mind in the present age; that is to say, of our habits of thinking directly and immediately about practice without considering at all that foundation of conscience, and enlarged experience, and philosophical enlightenment, on which good practice can alone be built.[2]

Wisdom in other countries and in other periods of this country has been held to include in itself a moral tendency and power, and much also of which it is not the purport to bear in the first instance on conduct, and many feelings and principles valuable not as instruments, but simply as being true and good. A philosopher, in the language of some generations, was a man who drew from his own mind and from the nature of things the laws of universal truth whereby alone phenomena can be explained. Nothing which is not an end in itself can be at once both fact and reason; and the merely mechanical and subservient requires something higher than it can supply to manifest the idea whereof it is the outward realization.

An idea of this kind has in truth the closest relation to men's feelings and affections. It was in this way that the philosophy of Socrates gained its proper and distinctive renown. Not because it was a mere classifying of external facts, but because it was drawn from the living substance of the human mind, instead of referring to abstractions and names which have nothing to do with the

[1] *Athenaeum* (18 June 1828). A disciple of Bentham, James Mill (1773-1836) founded the *Westminster Review* (1824-1907) as the organ of the philosophical radicals. Thus, the *Edinburgh*, the *Quarterly*, and the *Westminster Review* each represented a party, for whose adherents each disseminated the views peculiarly its own; and each, therefore, exerted a powerful but divisive influence upon public opinion in 1828.

[2] Uniting critical and speculative literature, this sketch confirms and illustrates the close connection, felt in Maurice's day, between literature and politics, and it allows Maurice, the critic, to emphasize the differences in literary kind. Despite opinion and impaired perception, glimpses of truth illuminate the contemporary scene, for Imagination prevails.

actual processes of our thoughts, desires, and convictions. It is, of course, possible to form scientific systems without reference to the testimony of consciousness;[3] and if these be sedulously and honestly framed, they will have a value of their own as means and materials. But the purport of those things which are the subjects of the science will be utterly beyond its domain, unless that shall have been traced out and subdued by a mind accustomed to meditate on itself. One kind of skill is requisite to put together the scattered leaves of Sibyl Nature,[4] and arrange in connected periods the piecemeal words and chaotic phraseology. Another, absolutely different and immeasurably higher, is necessary to interpret the language in which she writes, and expound her symbol characters.

But in our day and land a man earns the reputation of philosophy by simply generalising on facts, and for that purpose taking away from them everything which made them interesting to the agent. All the external business of the world has increased enormously in extent and activity. Experiment and mechanical invention have multiplied themselves in every department of industry. Earth, sea, and air have given up their secrets, and enriched mankind with all their powers. Every resource that nature contains has been investigated and applied: till the land has become one vast manufactory; the sea one broad highway of nations; every nook is the domain of labour, and every shore an emporium.

The mind of man is given up to these things: and production, and accumulation, have become the vocation of the world. Literature, too, partakes of this character: and the research for truth is no longer considered important, except inasmuch as it conducts to profit. We crowd to the temple, not that we may listen to the oracles or kneel before the altar; but to barter our souls at the tables of the money-changers. The curse, therefore, which smote Heliodorus[5] in the midst of his sacrilege, the same shall fall on us.

The world is sure enough to pay attention to its worldly wants. The necessities which we have in common with the beasts will always be of at least sufficient importance in ordinary eyes.

[3] In the sense of conscience, the arbiter of moral values.

[4] Nature is referred to as a woman posessing powers of prophecy and divination.

[5] See II Maccabees, Chapter 3. Heliodorus is sent by king Seleucus to take away the treasures deposited in the temple. He is struck by God, and healed by the prayers of the high priest.

It should be the business of literature to preserve and disseminate truth, with regard to those subjects which belong peculiarly to man, which constitute our essential humanity. To the philosopher is committed this task of teaching his age that there are many faculties in the mind besides those which are needful for the support of the body: that each has its peculiar object, beauty, morality, religion, truth; that to resolve any one into the other is to destroy so much of man's inheritance; and yet that, if any one be cultivated exclusively instead of independently of the rest, the whole will necessarily be ruined. Not only for the purpose of enforcing these truths is the philosopher appointed, but also for keeping alive on earth the conviction that, in the consciousness of these truths and in devotion to them, resides the genuine hope and glory of human nature: not for teaching religion, and religion in its highest and most perfect form, Christianity, as a thing totally cut off from our daily feeling and habitual conduct, but as including every department of thought, and all our duties, and those especially which are the laws of our most precious powers, and which flow from our relation to God.

A philosopher in this sense of the word Mr. Mill is not. He does not profess to love wisdom, but the consequences to which wisdom leads; and is, therefore, no more a philosopher than he who weds for money is a lover. The only wisdom which is of any value contains, in itself, the means of moral as well as intellectual excellence. It is essentially different from prudence; and an extended prudence is all which can be learned from the writings of this author, or is ever inculcated in them.

At the same time, he is often an acute and laborious authority; and the range of his general acquirements appears to be highly respectable, while his benevolence is obvious and delightful, and evidently proceeds from a higher source, and is supported by a stronger sanction than the author himself would be willing to recognise. His works, so far at least as is commonly known, are a volume of *The Elements of Political Economy* [1821], a *History of British India* [1818],[6] and several essays on Government and Legislation, in the Supplement to the *Encyclopaedia Britannica*.[7] If the author has produced any other works than these, it should

[6]On the strength of which, Mill obtained a high post in the service of the East India Company.

[7]Essays on *Government, Jurisprudence, Liberty of the Press,* etc. were reprinted from the Supplement to the *Encyclopaedia Britannica* in 1825, *An Essay on Government* being most widely read.

be remembered that by these alone he is here judged.

As mere compositions, they are marked by a niggard and dreary style, such that even the laurels of his fame will not suffice to conceal from a single eye the baldness they encircle. It seems to be the author's main effort to separate his subject into as many atoms as possible, and to put each of these into a sentence which will exactly hold it; and he takes a sedulous and perverse care to divest his little, lifeless, shapeless, fragmentary propositions of every accompaniment of sympathy or association, even the most completely justified by what goes before; so as to secure the want of all unity of impression from the whole.

This is a great defect; and akin to it is another: Mr. Mill never brings before us his view of any point by an image; which may at once make the subject plainer than whole pages of mere argumentation, and by remaining fixed in the mind, may for ever serve to recall the reason which it has originally illustrated. Does Mr. Mill really believe that the column is the weaker or the less majestic, because the primroses grow around its base; that the armour is the more frail, because it is embossed with gold; or, that the Damascus sabre[8] will smite the less surely, for its flowery fragrance?

Like the fountain, which nourishes the roots of the oak, a feeling lies deep and fresh at the root of all valuable moral truths. It goes along with them in all their progress; and if we find that which professes to be such a truth unaccompanied by this inward life, we may be sure that it is either an error, or the produce of some other mind than that which presented it to us; even as if we saw a tree on a dry spot of the desert, we might be certain that it either was utterly useless, or had been brought thither from some more generous soil. In ethics, love accompanies intelligence; and when a man is writing on these subjects, affection will show itself, now in tracing out a thousand analogies, now in bringing rapidly together many particulars, all welded into one by the fervour of the soul; and, again, by perpetually recurring from the individual proposition to the general feeling which alone gives it importance.

It is easy to say that all this is so much injury done to the logical excellence of the style: but to harmonise logical perfection with strength of sentiment is the task and the prerogative of

---

[8] A sword ornamented with a thin ribbon of wrought iron coiled round, and welded to the hilt.

philosophers and men of genius; and, moreover, if part of a composition brings everyone, whose sympathies are healthy, into a certain state of consciousness, with which the tone of the remainder of the author's speculations is totally at variance, however fitted it may be to any arbitrary canons of the schools, human nature will trample on schools and scholars and proclaim that the logic of rhetoricians[9] is very different from the logic of the mind.

Such seem to us the radical defects of Mr. Mill's style. On the whole, it wants both ease and strength. It is, as nearly as possible, the style of Euclid's *Elements*[10] adapted to subjects for which Euclid never would have used it. Dry, harsh, and prickly, it would be utterly unendurable but that there is enough of real information conveyed in it to compensate for much annoyance. Grapes do sometimes grow on thorns, and figs on thistles; though now and then the grapes are sour and the figs, like those sold in the streets of Constantinople, are cried with rather excessive ostentation.[11]

There would nevertheless be something manly and simple in this writer's compositions but for the affectation which is exhibited in many occasional phrases, a sort of Utilitarian coxcombry, and professorial pretension. Such modes of speech as "the matter of evil", and "portion of discourse"; and the formulas (they occur in every page of Mr. Mill's writings) "either a thing is white, or it is black. If white, then, &c., if black, then something else," and so forth; all these are mere pedantries, worthy only of a school-boy in the lowest class of the Utilitarian philosophy — a neophyte in the outer court of the temple of the economic goddess. Yet we believe these absurdities may help to win admirers and proselytes. For when the merely getting by rote a few simple phrases and sentences of this kind, and the employment of them in all companies, will gain for anyone the reputation of profoundness, it would be strange indeed if many did not avail them-

[9]We must be satisfied for the present to take *Rhetoric* in Dr. Whately's sense of "Argumentative Composition." [Maurice's note]

Richard Whately (1787-1863), author of *Logic* (1826) and *Rhetoric* (1828).

[10]A treatise on geometry.

[11]"In the name of the prophet, Figs!" Mr. Mill's prophet, however, is not Mahomet, but Mr. Bentham. [Maurice's note]

From his son's *Autobiography* (Chapter II) one may add that, encumbered thus prophetically, James Mill's "standard of morals was Epicurean inasmuch as it was utilitarian, taking as the exclusive test of right and wrong, the tendency of actions to produce pleasure or pain. But he had (and this was the Cynic element) scarcely any belief in pleasure. . . ."

selves of so easy a *gradus ad philosophiam.*[12]

It has been said already that Mr. Mill has knowledge sufficient to make him — in spite of these drawbacks — a valuable author. If we did not think him an influential writer, we should not now be examining the character of his works. But it is observable that little of his knowledge is his own. He is not, indeed, one of the pedants who put their minds into their books instead of putting their books into their minds.

But neither is he one of the thinkers who, instead of keeping books in their minds as they came from their authors, recompose them there with a thousand new illustrations, strong connections, and nice dependencies. Take the system of the human mind of Locke,[13] the theory of religion of Hume,[14] the principles of government and legislation of Bentham,[15] and the political economy of Ricardo;[16] deprive these of all which made them peculiarly the property of their inventors, of all their air of originality, of all their individual lineaments, and join them together in one mass, and you have the creed of the historian of British India. But many of the doctrines which he holds have undoubtedly been stated by him more clearly than by anyone else: and in his great work he has applied them to a wide range of subjects, and supported them in appearance by such a multiplicity of facts, that it certainly deserves to be held among the oracular books of the sect.

The *History of British India* [1818] is clearly distinguishable, though not divisible, into two parts. The one relates to England and Englishmen, the other to India and its natives. Of the former of these portions we need say but little. It is in general executed with ability and knowledge. For the author's system of human nature, though professing to be universal, is drawn from the circumstances of modern Europe; and the vesture fits tolerably well

[12]In this context, there is ironical humour in Maurice's use of the phrase by which Coleridge distinguished between Reason and Understanding.

[13]Knowledge, for Locke, was based on experiment, experience, and association.

[14]From an observable design in nature, Hume inferred a God intelligent but not necessarily good.

[15]Bentham legislated upon the maxim of the greatest happiness of the greatest number.

[16]David Ricardo (1771-1823), author of *The Principles of Political Economy and Taxation* (1817), concerned himself with the causes determining the distribution of wealth.

the form for which it was intended — infinitely better at least than it would adapt itself to any other. His observations on commercial questions are commonly excellent: and his mode of analysing the different measures and institutions of British states-manship is full of acuteness.

Even in these we could have wished for some more earnest enforcing of national duty, some stronger evidences of faith in the possibility of human virtue. But if there is any subject in discussing which the want of that faith is excusable, it is un-doubtedly the recent history of English Parliaments and Minis-ters. His scalpel is practised in the laying open men's motives; and if he is too much predisposed to find the parts diseased, he is at all events an unsparing operator when they really are so. We should probably not be inclined to make the same use of Mr. Mill's political discoveries and demonstrations as he would do. But they are curious and valuable to every benevolent reformer who has accustomed his mind to trace and to lament the influ-ence of bad institutions on national well-being.

But with regard to that more difficult division of this writer's labours which refers to Hindustan, we can give no such applause. It seems to us that his views on this subject are fundamentally and desperately wrong. He has in no one instance made the slightest approach to an understanding of the Hindu polity.

To comprehend the principles and mode of thought which prevail among any people, it is necessary to seize the idea on which their social system is founded. In every community which has antiquity and a national life of its own, such an idea has existed, the mould for the mind of the society, sometimes par-tially realised in institutions, sometimes partially manifested in great changes, sometimes lost for a period amid internal tumults or, perhaps, destroyed for ever by subjection to foreigners. But to grasp this is to hold the clue which alone can guide us to full intelligence of the religion, the laws, the literature, the primary institutions of a people. To select some of its results, and to judge them by rules totally independent of the cause from which those results arose is to take security for our own ignorance, and to give evidence of nothing but our own folly. This has been done by the author whom we are now considering; and this has vitiated all his reasonings.

The more difficult and more interesting points in the subject of his great work are almost all of them thus perverted. Nor is there a single object looked at in the light of any other master-thought than that of the universal propensity of mankind to pursue what appears to them their own interest. The writer[17] sees in the institution of castes, and in all the laws which are explicable by that institution (but which he does not so explain), only the proofs that a people may be deluded to their own misery. He does not attempt to understand the historical idea of Hindu society, which is necessary for expounding all its phenomena.

Neither do we profess to understand it. But we at least see its necessity. The difficulties of the subject may, *perhaps* (we speak in doubt and humility), be explained by supposing that the higher castes, the priestly and the warlike, were in some distant age the invaders and conquerors of India. One of those armies of soldiers, conducted by the wisdom of priests, which at one period or other of a remote antiquity has overrun the whole world, has produced changes, political and religious, as important to mankind as the greatest of the physical convulsions of the earth have been to the material globe. This notion (we avow it to be nothing more) as regards India, would give a purport and ulterior interest to the wonderful fact of the sovereigns of that country having assumed to themselves, and still retaining, the rack-rents of the whole Peninsula. We confess that the hypothesis mentioned above, which we have no pretension to claim as our own, is the only one which occurs to our minds as indicating a source copious and remote enough to permit the deduction from it of all those wide and long and powerful currents which now mark the social surface of India.

But be this as it may, all we contend for is that a grave, a learned, an able author, such as undoubtedly is Mr. Mill, was bound to furnish some explanation of the mysteries and hieroglyphics painted on the walls, amid which he leads us temporarily to inhabit. If he merely copies the inscription instead of translating it, he does not fulfill his task. Or, to take a kindred image, if he affixes to the words which were written in one language the meaning which those sounds indicate in another, he commits an error not glorious to himself and mischievous to the majority of his readers.

The one object of the long and elaborate chapters on the Hindus and of many subsequent casual allusions, is to determine the point in the scale of what the writer terms civilisation, at

[17]Mill.

which the people he speaks of, stood. But it is painful to feel, throughout, the impossibility of discovering in his pages any clear account of what *civilisation* is. Many of those things which thinkers of all parties would regard as helping to constitute civilisation are, by him, uniformly spoken of as being merely its evidences. Many which, in our eyes, are accidental peculiarities are, in his, the strongest proofs of it; and those which are held for its essence and life, by the believers in man's religious and moral nature are, by him, either totally omitted, or treated with some indication of careless contempt. It seems probable that, if all he has said on the subject were brought together, he would be found to place the good and beautiful of a nation in the knowledge and practice of sound political economy and in an improved judicial system — to the entire exclusion of everything which comes home to men's feelings, of all improvement in the sense of duty, in reverence for truth, in love to God and man.[18]

We are inclined to think that the majority of the political mistakes of this reasoner, though the natural outgrowth of an erroneous and unhappy system of human nature, could not have existed to such a degree without an inattention to the spirit of history, a kindred product of the same system. Is it not melancholy that an *Essay on Government* should have been written, however concise and compendious, in which we find no more than one or two cursory allusions to the experience of nations? And is not this fact a symptom of a general tendency to turn away the eye from all that is necessarily different in the circumstances of different communities? To shut from our contemplation that inner life of society which is perpetually working outward, and flinging off the slough and decay of its body; and as constantly drawing in to feed itself with, and assimilate them to its own nature, the resources and materials that surround it?[19]

There is a growth and progress of a people which acts from an interior law of its own, and makes the application to it at any

[18]Maurice again emphasizes the attributes of the genuine poet: duty, in the sense of moral obligation, reverence for truth, and love of God and neighbour.

[19]Social development, like the growth of plants, is organic. Maurice has chosen his analogy from Coleridge: "Lo! — with the rising sun it commences its outward life and enters into open communion with all the elements, at once assimilating them to itself and to each other. . . . Lo! — at the touch of light how it returns an air akin to light, and yet with the same pulse effectuates its own secret growth, still contracting to fix what expanding it had refined." *Lay Sermons* (1852), Appendix B, p. 77.

period, of a merely abstract theory, a folly and an impossibility. Any man who should directly assert that the same institutions are applicable to all countries at every time, to the North American Indians, to the Arabs, the Hottentots, the Chinese, the English — would not be a man to be answered, but one to be put in a straight-waistcoat. Yet, the reasonings of the *Essay on Government* are as universal as those of geometry and, if good at all, would be just as valid arguments for a Negro or an Eskimo, as for a Parisian or a Prussian. To rest satisfied, therefore, with it as with a sound political system, is quietly to repose on the pillow of an absurdity.

The chapter of the *History* on the literature of India, ought to have been one of the highest interest and value. There are few things of the kind more curious, than the absence of all history, the general extravagance of the poetry, in connection with the occasional subtlety and sublimity of the philosophical doctrines in the books of the Brahmins. Mr. Mill treats the whole subject as contemptible. His criticism on the Hindu works of imagination is probably not much too severe, though it exhibits no evidence whatsoever of critical science.

But it is scarcely conceivable by what extravagance of Voltairian empiricism he should have been led to write as he has done about Indian philosophy. We doubt not that, with some exceptions, it is absurd and stupid; and that the better portions of it are little understood or cherished by the vast majority of the Brahmins. But how did the Vedantic theory ever arise among such a people?[20] Mr. Mill pretends to bring evidence that refined abstract speculations have always flourished among rude nations; but he brings no testimonies — none, at least, the vagueness of which does not make it entirely nugatory — to the existence of metaphysical science in any barbarous country except, indeed, where it has been transplanted from the Athenian garden, or copied from the paintings of the Stoa.[21]

Nor can we be satisfied with the still more shallow device of asserting that the "propensity to abstract speculations is the natural result of the state of the human mind in a rude and ignorant age" (*History of British India,* vol. ii, p. 70, 8vo.

---

[20]The Brahmins, the highest priestly caste among the Hindus, based their philosophy on the Vedas, four of the most ancient sacred books in the world.

[21]The colonnade in the market-place in Athens, adorned with frescoes by famous artists.

edition);[22] or with the ludicrous impropriety of the attempt to support this statement by the authority of Condillac,[23] who merely says that children early learn to class many objects together from observation of their outward resemblances. Mr. Mill pretends that the Vedantic doctrine is utterly despicable and worthless, both as given by Sir William Jones[24] and by Sir James Mackintosh. It would be easy for Mr. Mill to say the same of Plato. But one assertion is worth just as much as another; and we confess we cannot conceive how such a belief can have arisen, except from the partial perversion of some early and holy tradition, or from the force of a powerful and subtle mind long accustomed to brood over its own consciousness.

Now the difficulty, and it appears in our eyes a great one, is to discover in what way a theory so remote and transcendant (however erroneous; and we are convinced, that if we have it in its integrity, it is erroneous) can have been united to such gross and miserable follies as form the mass of Sanskrit learning. However, we can now pursue no further the examination of the chapter on literature, and must leave to the judgment of its readers, its heap of irrelevant, ill-arranged, and uncompared authorities, its careless condemnation of things which the writer has not taken the trouble to comprehend, and its grave quotation from Voltaire, of the precious opinion that the poetry of the Old Testament is completely worthless. But we must turn to say a few words of a chapter on religion which is about as valuable, when compared with the theology of Isaiah, as is the poetry of the *Pucelle*[25] when weighed against the book of Job.

We are very anxious that nothing we say should tend to excite a religious clamour against the writings now before us. To our fear of abetting this theological fury we would give up anything except candour. And we trust that we shall save ourselves from being accomplices in so odious a result by premising that, so far as we have seen, this writer has never said anything against the truth of Christianity. If he had avowed himself to be a Deist or an atheist, we should still feel nothing but regret and should

[22]Maurice is using the edition in six volumes (1826).

[23]The author of *Traité des sensations* (1754), and thus the founder of sensationalism.

[24]An English oriental scholar (1746-94) who, with Sir Charles Wilkins (1749-1836) pioneered the study of Sanskrit and noted its affinity with other languages in the Indo-European family.

[25]*La Pucelle* (1755), Voltaire's burlesque epic on the subject of Joan of Arc.

endeavour, as earnestly as possible, to show the cruelty, the folly, the criminality, of persecuting any man's conscience.

The author attempts to account for the existence of religion in the world (independent of revelation) by saying that, "prior to experience and instruction, there is a propensity in the imagination to endow with life whatever we behold in motion; or, in general, whatever appears to be the cause of any event. A child beats the inanimate object by which it has been hurt, and caresses that by which it has been gratified". Now, in the first place, is this conduct on the part of children anything more than imitation? If not, the analogy goes for nothing. But does the author really think that so universal and so permanent a power as (unrevealed) religion is to be accounted for by a sentence about a child whipping a foot-stool? And in the process which he describes, whereby from such an origin religion grows up, till at last the "ingenuity of fear and desire" invents "a higher strain of flattery" and men find out the unity of God (see *History of British India,* vol. i, p. 295, 8vo. edition) "in this process, can a calm and candid mind discover causes sufficient to produce all the different religions of the world, and all the strange varieties, idolatry, Pantheism, and pure Theism?"[26]

No; whatever may be said as to natural religion by those who exaggerate what needs no adventitious importance, the value, namely, of revelation, or by those who depreciate it from indifference to religion of all kinds, there must be at the root of the human mind a propensity, the strongest and best portion of our birthright, to believe in something higher and earlier than nature. The trouble is not to account for the existence of religion, but for the imperfection of it. And nothing can solve the difficulty but our knowledge of the feebleness of all the faculties of savages, and of the slightness of any tendency among them to refer particulars to universals, and exchange notions for ideas. To prove that religious feeling often exists in no shape but that of debasing superstition, is not to prove that man had better be without religion, but that his whole nature stands in need of improvement. Improve mankind, and pure religion grows up along with their moral growth, and is its most perfect and precious produce.

[26]Pantheism (O. E. D.) may suggest (a) the worship of many gods, or (b) the doctrine that God is everything and everything is God (implying a denial of the personality and transcendence of God).

Theism is the belief in one God as creator and supreme ruler of the universe, without denial of revelation.

It strikes us as extremely curious that Mr. Mill should not have been more impressed and interested by the strange mixture of true and false, of good and evil, found in the books of Indian theology, from which he quotes so largely. There are fragments of the most sublime Deism,[27] and others of a beautiful Pantheism, mixed in wonderful confusion and in melancholy contrast with all that is vilest and meanest in a miserable system of idolatry. How did these heterogeneous particles coalesce? How did the dust of corruption and the Spirit of God thus meet together? Whence this mingling of life and death? No such question as this occurs to the writer. It never suggests itself to him that a great truth cannot have been the contemporaneous produce of the same mind as a host of errors, all of which that truth excludes. He does not inquire; he does not hesitate; he starts no hypothesis; much less does he search diligently till he has found the original key to the mystery. But he carelessly throws aside the whole matter with the observation that improvement in the language of religion is no evidence of improvement in the idea: and most certainly it is no evidence with regard to those who employ it, but the strongest with regard to those who invented it.

Had we space at command, could we publish a tithe of the pages in one of Mr. Mill's volumes, we would willingly consider these subjects at far greater length. As it is, we must now quit them; and we should much regret if, in doing so, we were to leave our readers under an impression more unfavourable to this teacher than is our own. It is natural, in examining literary works of a speculative character, to dwell on those points with regard to which we differ from the author.

But we beg our readers to remember, that we have judged Mr. Mill by the very highest of all standards, namely, by contrasting his performance with ideal excellence.[28] He is obviously a person of unwearied diligence, of great acuteness, of a well-compacted and highly-disciplined intellect; and above all, of a strong and large benevolence. The last of these merits we perhaps estimate at least as highly as some of those who would be louder and more indiscriminate in their applause.

Nor do we overlook the merit of this writer in opposing him-

---

[27]"Natural religion", or the belief in the existence of God with a rejection of revelation (O. E. D.).

[28]Of imaginatively creative men like Wordsworth and Shelley. Compare XII, 1; XII, 14; XIII, 2; XIII, 18.

self, amid such a system as that which now prevails in England, to the many misdeeds of power. But such is our impression of the importance of principles, and of the principles more especially with regard to which we differ from Mr. Mill, that we should have outraged the strongest sense of duty by concealing or qualifying our dissent from his doctrine. And no fear of being called what we should most abhor to be, persecutors, that is, and bigots, shall prevent us from raising our voices against a system which, in our view, would make reason, imagination, truth, and benevolence, mere instruments for supplying those wants which we have in common with the brutes,[29] instead of their being the powers which wear the image of God, and are designed to raise us towards Him.

[29]Maurice's last word in *Sketches* refers to Coleridge's *gradus ad philosophiam* as he opposes the reduction of reason to instinctual understanding.

APPENDICES

Maurice on Coleridge

A

(i) [Coleridge's Influence on Englishmen]

A number of persons who had cared little for any interests but their own class or private interests, began to think of the greatest happiness of the greatest number; nay, to bestir themselves for the promotion of that happiness, sometimes in ways which [Bentham] had suggested, sometimes in ways which he would have disapproved. Many who had an intense dislike to Methodism, the least possible sympathy with the old English devotions, yet spoke in their own way of an Eternal and Infinite Being, all good and benevolent, who was seeking the greatest happiness of His creatures. So that one branch of the nineteenth century philosophy grew and flourished, in spite of itself, under this protection. How was it with the other branch?

Coleridge had participated as little as possible in the Methodist excitement. Though the son of a clergyman he had shaken off the habits of his childhood. He had attached himself to Priestley[1] and the Unitarians. Their doctrine respecting a universal Father had a mighty attraction for him. He was ready to preach it in all the towns of England. If he felt himself repelled at times by their coldness, at times by their want of logic, his political anticipations were a refuge from the first; he could find in Hartley's beautiful harmonies a charm for his intellect as well as his affections. The road from Hartley's sympathetic wires to the all-embracing godhead of Spinoza was not a long one. How far more satisfying was that "divine drunkenness" than the dogmatism of men who spoke about an exclusive oneness, a negation of plurality! Then came the anguish of parting with those dreams which he had cherished [the French revolution], of a time when

[1] Joseph Priestley (1733-1804), Unitarian minister and author of *Essay on the First Principles of Government* (1768), in which he advocated the happiness of the majority as the basis of social organisation, a theory taken up and developed by Bentham.

> Wisdom should teach her lore
> In the low huts of them who toil and groan;
> And, conquering by her happiness alone,
> France should compel the nations to be free,
> Till love and joy looked round and called the
>   earth their own.[2]

Kant must have been indeed an ice-bucket to one who had just come out of this cauldron. All demonstrations of the being of God proved alike futile! The speculative reason always deceiving itself! A doubt whether there is any passage from ideas to reality! Coleridge has given in his *Literary Life* one hint respecting this crisis which is worth much more for his biography than most of its direct narratives. He learnt, he says, that if he could believe in God other difficulties would be nothing to him. That was the infinite difficulty. But he discovered that it was also the infinite necessity. He could believe nothing till he had this ground of belief. To feel this rock at his feet — to know that it was a rock — he had need to be shown something also of what he himself was. There was awakened in him a

> Sense of past youth, and manhood come in vain,
> And genius given, and knowledge won in vain;
> And all which he had culled in wood-walks wild,
> And all which patient toil had reared, and all
> Commune with friends had opened out — but flowers
> Strewed on his corse and borne upon his bier,
> In the same coffin, for the self-same grave.[3]

By such fearful experiences, combining with the studies of his previous life, Coleridge was brought to the conviction that the words which Englishmen had been wont to repeat, which he had been taught in his infancy, were not blasphemous, damnable words. There was a point at which the old faith of his land intersected the most modern philosophy of another land. The demand for Being by Plato, by Spinoza, by the Germans since Kant, was not an idle demand. The *I am that I am* who spoke to the Hebrew shepherd awakened it and answered it. The demand for Unity by philosophical and religious schools was not an idle

---

[2] An adaptation of Coleridge's *France: An Ode* (59-63).

[3] Adapted from Coleridge's *To William Wordsworth* (69-75).

demand. The name which was written upon the Christian child satisfied it. The belief in a Father, which Priestley and the Unitarians had inculcated, was a deep and true belief. But that it might be real and practical, that it might not mock men with the idlest hope, there must be a union between the Father and His children; there must be a redemption from evil. That redemption from evil fully justified all the protests of those who had most consciousness of evil, against a mere scheme of optimism. It could never justify them in making evil a ground or starting-point in their ethics. The emancipation and purification of the conscience must imply that there is a conscience to be emancipated and purified. The belief in a Spirit who awakens the human will or spirit must imply that there is a spirit or will to be awakened.[4]

"The greatest happiness of the greatest numbers" appeared to Coleridge to be one of those vague generalities which Bentham was in the habit of imputing to all thinkers who did not agree with him, and to many who did. Happiness, he said, must be either defined, or treated as the unknown quantity; if you begin to poll men, in order to know what they count happiness, you engage in a hopeless task; if you decide for them what is happiness, you introduce a tyrannical dogmatism; you are obliged to return to the old search for the duty of each person which you supposed that you were rid of. He did not perhaps see how much was implied in the very vagueness of this idea. Those who supposed that the reason of man was to discover what happiness was, and that there was a happiness for all human beings, might approach much nearer to his doctrine of a universal reason than they knew themselves. Those who had been baffled in their experiments to discover what was happiness in their own case, or to make other men understand what was happiness in theirs, might come nearer to the belief in a standard of good, even in a Being who sets forth that standard, and is that standard, than was at all indicated by the terms in which they expressed their theory. Theories are not much for Englishmen: habits of mind are much more.

There came, however, a time [between 1815 and 1830] . . . when those who had been seeking and questioning began to systematize. The disciples of Bentham were not content any longer merely to announce a maxim and denounce evils. They became fierce and dogmatic. All doctrines were scorned

[4]Experience and study led Coleridge to believe in God, while his conscience informed him of the Trinitarian character of that God.

which could not be brought under their formula. The whole universe had been made, or must be made, according to their formula. If those who had profited by Coleridge's teaching had not been a much smaller and more insignificant body, there would have been the same danger of their becoming an arrogant and exclusive school. Coleridge himself was always promising a great work called *Logo-Sophia,* which might perhaps settle all questions, and be a complete organon of philosophy and theology . . . .

The real *Logo-Sophia* of Coleridge is contained in his *Lay Sermons,* which show that the wisdom of God, who through the prophets set forth moral and political principles to the Jews, is setting forth the same principles through them to Englishmen; in his *Aids to Reflection,* wherein he awakens young men to ask themselves whether that divine Wisdom is not speaking to *them* — whether the maxims of prudence and the messages to the conscience do not proceed from Him — whether there is not a will in them which can only be free when it is obeying the motions of a higher Will.[5]

The political movements in England which coincided with those in France after the revolution of 1830 had a vast influence upon the development of the doctrine which Bentham had preached. Many of his disciples found themselves called from their studies to practical life — from protesting against abuses to experiments for removing them. Such times are trying to any opinion, as much from the suspicion and disappointments of those who hope, as from the opposition of those who fear, its success. Obstacles of experience that have not been foreseen are found to hinder the application of dogmas; official coldness succeeds to private fervour; the most enlightened and honest begin to perceive facts and even principles of which they have not taken account. On the whole, however, it cannot be doubted that the belief of utility as the sufficient maxim for states and individuals was the predominant one of those years [1830-1850].

Some of its results, rather than any dislike to the theory, made the Conservative party in the land inquire whether there was not some opposing principle which might enable them to combat it. For a while the name of Coleridge acquired a certain respect and popularity. His maxims were patronized by distinguished men, even by the newspapers. It was thought that they might do serv-

[5] Coleridge's writings persuaded Englishmen that God was their Guide.

ice in some civil and ecclesiastical conflicts . . . . [But] soon it was discovered that Coleridge was not the writer from whom a principle could be most conveniently obtained for such purposes. Though an earnest defender, in spite of early prejudices, of the national ritual, and though more ready than most to accept it as a gift to the nation from the past, he did not regard it chiefly as a tradition — he did not submit to it mainly because authority was in its favour . . . . We may acknowledge that [Rationalist Benthamite utilitarians] were perfectly right in their conclusion that Coleridge could give them no help in maintaining their position — that no one had done more to prove it an unsafe and untenable one.[6]

Maurice, *Moral and Metaphysical Philosophy* (1872), ii, 688 ff.

(ii) [Coleridge's Practical Influence on England]

Some of our readers may be astonished that we assert for Coleridge also the title of a practical as contradistinguished from a professional philosopher. Was he not essentially a Transcendentalist? Was it not his main, though unsuccessful, desire to recommend Kant to his countrymen? Did he not learn much from Schelling? It is perfectly true that the poet, who had been filled with all the fears and hopes with which the French revolution inspired young men, who had dreamt of an American pantisocracy, who had seen his visions vanish and Napoleon enthroned, did at a certain time of his life become a metaphysician. The reason and the effect of that course are expressed with the bitterness of self-reproach in his ode on *Dejection* —

> So not to think of what I needs must feel,
>   But to be still and patient all I can,
> And haply by abstruse research to steal
>   From my own nature all the natural man,
>   This was my sole resource, my only plan,
> Till what befits a part infects the whole,
> And now has almost grown the habit of my soul.[1]

[6] Reason dictated that happiness lay in obedience to "a higher Will", and not in human systems.

[1] *Dejection: An Ode* (VI: 87-93), apparently quoted from memory.

Nevertheless, this abstruse student wrote in newspapers about the events of the war, the conduct and character of our ministers, and the government of France. And when he did begin in his *Friend* to make some use of his German lore, so far from producing a systematic philosophical treatise, he gave his critics good ground for complaining that his Essays were fragmentary and upon all possible subjects. . . . Those, indeed, who learnt, and still learn, from the *Friend,* perceive that it had one main purpose; that whether Coleridge discussed questions of art or questions of ethics, or — what have the largest place in the book — questions of politics, he was seeking to distinguish between those principles which are universal, which belong to one man as much as another, and those rules and maxims which are generalized from experience.

Having this end in view he accepted Kant's distinction between the understanding and the reason as of inestimable worth. That distinction explained, he thought, the confusions into which the authors of the French declaration of rights and their English admirers had fallen. They had mixed together the universal and the particular, the laws of Reason and the deductions of the Understanding.[2] The maxims belonging to the one sphere, which were local and temporary, were invested with the sacredness and largeness of the other. Therefore national limits had been effaced, all customs, traditions, beliefs, had been treated as unnecessary. Yet the universal principles had not been asserted. A false universality had been substituted for the true. An imperial universality had been the outcome of the universal equality and fraternity. So Coleridge vindicated the experimental maxims of Burke, while he vindicated also the deep underground principles of society which Burke had been afraid to look into. He believed that these ought to be investigated; that the politician must recognize them if he is not to sail without chart or compass; that the man must recognize them if he is to be an honest and intelligent citizen.

What we have said may help to remove the impression that any part of Coleridge's influence arose from the unpractical qualities of his mind . . . .

Maurice, *Moral and Metaphysical Philosophy* (1872), ii, 665-66.

[2] Coleridge applied the *gradus ad philosophiam* to show wherein the French revolution had failed.

B

(i) [Coleridge's Influence on J. C. Hare]

Some of Coleridge's contemporaries had been led, like Hare[1] himself, to believe "that man is not an animal carrying about a soul, but a spiritual being with an animal nature, who, when he has sunk lowest into that nature, still has thoughts and recollections of a home to which he belongs, and from which he has wandered". But they had also been told "that the age of Theology had passed, and the age of Science begun."

"If Science has become Omniscience," [they thought], "can it not interpret that cry for a Living God which still goes up from human hearts whether there is a Theology or not?"

"It was not, therefore, because these weary seekers wanted a compromise between the old and the new,[2] because they were afraid to follow truth whithersoever it led them, but because they were sure that unless they pushed their enquiries further, they should be obliged to retrace their steps, to unlearn all they had learnt, to sink back into materialism, to believe in Mammon — though they believed nothing else — that they welcomed the voice of [Coleridge] who said to them, "What you are feeling after is that Father's house which the men of the old time spoke of."

"Beneath all strange mystical utterances . . . they heard this practical message from his lips, [and] they saw that he could not have received it or proclaimed it unless the whole man within him had passed through a tremendous convulsion . . . .[3] They discovered that it was not merely his reason which had demanded God as its foundation, but that he had been compelled by the feebleness of his will, by the sense of moral evil, to cry out to that God, in the old language,

"Be merciful to me a sinner."

[1] J. C. Hare (1795-1835), Archdeacon of Lewes, and Maurice's tutor at Cambridge.

[2] Between theology and science.

[3] Conscience effected a conversion.

This explains Julius Hare's "unshaken attachment" to Coleridge. Hare "owed" to Coleridge "probably more than to any
other man [the fact] "that he was able to trace the path which
connects human learning with divine, the faith of one age with
the faith of another, the sense of man's grandeur with the sense
of his pettiness and sinfulness . . . He [learned] that the Reformation had removed the great obstacle to unity, by holding forth
the actual belief and knowledge of God, as possible for all men;
he [learned] that philology and criticism, which become dangerous when they are not free, will, if they are honestly used, be
found instruments — subordinate, but still most precious instruments — in restoring faith in God's word, and fellowship among
his children.[4]

Maurice, "An Introduction, Explanatory of [Hare's] Position in
        the Church with Reference to the Parties which Divide
        It." In J. C. Hare, *Charges to the Clergy of the Arch-
        deaconry of Lewes* (1856), i, xxi ff.

[4]Coleridge taught Hare that unity is possible.

C

(i) [Coleridge's Influence on Maurice]

There are persons who can feel no affection for a book unless
they can associate it with a living man. I am not sure whether I
labour under this incapacity, but I own that the books of Mr.
Coleridge are mainly interesting to me as the biography of one
who passed through the struggles of the age to which we are
succeeding, and who was able, after great effort and much
sorrow, to discover a resting-place. Those juvenile poems which
exhibit him to us when he was seeking in Unitarianism a refuge
from the flatness and the falsehood of a mere State Christianity;
the fierce and magnificent ode in which he sees the old European
world of convention and oppression falling to pieces, and rejoices
in the sight; the noble recantation of his hopes from republican
ascendancy; his ode to Despondency, embodying so perfectly the
feelings of a man who, after the disappointment of all practical
hopes had sought in meditation for deliverance and rest, and then
on returning to the actual world had found its glory departed and
his capacities of enjoyment dead; — these poems have always
seemed to me so intensely and painfully real, and so expressive of
what thousands of minds in different measures must have been
experiencing, that I do not suppose I have ever done justice to
any of them, merely as a work of art. I do not think there is
anything inconsistent in this acknowledgment with the belief
that in him, as in every great poet, the exercise of the creative
faculty implied self-forgetfulness, and the power of passing
beyond the region of personal experience. No one can utter the
thoughts of other men as well as his own, can be in any degree
the spokesman of his time, to whom this quality does not belong.
But it consists, I should imagine, nearly always with much of
inward suffering. The person who enters most into what a
number of others are experiencing, does, in the strictest and
liveliest sense, experience it himself. On these points, however, I
have no right to speak and, if I speak ignorantly, you must
remember that I merely pretend to tell you what my own

impressions have been, not to make them a standard for other readers. Your father's greater poems, such as the Ancient Mariner, and Christabel, seem undoubtedly to belong to the region of the pure imagination. But I question whether I should be as much interested as I am even in these, if I did not discover in them many veins and fibres which seem to me to connect them with his personal being; if they did not help me to read more clearly the history of his mind, and therein the history of our time.

And as I have never learnt to separate his poetical genius from himself, so I fear I have been as little able to appreciate him formally and abstractedly in the character of a philosopher. In his Friend[1] I seem to discover the very same man whom I had known amidst the storms of the revolutionary period. Nor do I find him less impatient of mere rules and decrees than he was then; only the impatience has taken a new form. He has been convinced that society is a reality, that it would not become at all more real by being unmade and reconstructed, and therefore he has begun to inquire what are the grounds of its reality, and how we may be preserved from making it into a fiction and a falsehood. That this inquiry is complete and satisfactory I do not affirm, I rejoice to think that it is not; I believe, if it had been more complete, it would not be half so profitable as it has been and is likely to be for generations to come. Its merit is that it is an inquiry, that it shows us what we have to seek for, and that it puts us into a way of seeking. Hence it was and is particularly offensive to more than one class of persons. The mere Destructive complains that it recognizes the worth of that which ought to be swept away. The mere Conservative is indignant, because it will not assume existing rules and opinions as an ultimate basis, but aims at discovering their meaning and their foundation. The man of compromises is most bitter, because it assumes that the statesman has some other law of conduct than that of sailing with the wind. The mere Englishman is angry to find the common topics of the day, taxes, libels, bombardments of Copenhagen, not treated of as they are treated in his favourite journals. The man of Abstractions cannot understand what such topics have to do with a scientific book. This combination of enemies, with the advantage which each derives from being able to speak

[1] *The Friend, a Literary, Moral, and Political Journal,* 27 parts 1809-1810; reissued 1812 and 1818.

of the book as "neither one thing nor the other," is quite sufficient to explain any measure of unpopularity which it may have
met with. To account for the power which it has exerted in spite
of these disadvantages, and many others of an outward kind
which I need not hint at in writing to you; to explain how a
book, which is said to be utterly unpractical, has wrought a
change in men's minds upon the most practical subjects, how a
book, which is said to have no sympathy with the moving spirit
of this age, should have affected the most thoughtful of our
young men; this is a work of greater difficulty, which I hope that
some of our reviewers will one day undertake. I am not attempting to solve any such problems, but am merely accounting for its
influence upon my own mind, an influence mainly owing to
those very peculiarities which seem to have impaired or destroyed its worth in the opinions of wiser people. For this, at
least, I am thankful, that this book, so far from diminishing my
interest in those which treat of the same subject, or tempting me
to set Mr. Coleridge up as the one teacher upon it, has enabled
me to honour others of the most different kind, belonging to our
own and to former times, which I otherwise should not have
understood, and might, through ignorance and self-conceit, have
undervalued; above all, to reverence the facts of history, and to
believe that the least perversion of them, for the sake of getting a
moral from them, is at once a folly and a sin.

And it seems to me that I have found help of a similar kind to
this in a different department of thought from that still more
irregular work, the *Biographia Literaria*.[2] If a young man in this
age is much tormented by the puzzles of society, and the
innumerable systems by which men have sought to get rid of
them, he is haunted almost as much as the different problems of
criticism, by a sense of the connexion between his own life and
the books, which he reads, by theories about the nature and
meaning of this connexion, by authoritative dogmas respecting
the worth or worthlessness of particular poems and paintings, by
paradoxical rebellions against these dogmas, by questions as to
the authority of antiquity and the distinct province of our time,
by attempts to discover some permanent laws of art, by
indignant assertions of its independence of all laws. A person
cannot have observed himself or his contemporaries with any
attention, nay, he can scarcely read over the rude statement of

[2] Published in 1817.

these difficulties which I have just made, without feeling how intricately they are involved with our thoughts upon some of the very highest subjects. To say that we do not need to understand ourselves upon these critical questions, that it is of no importance to have principles in reference to them, is merely to say that we ought not to meddle with them at all. A person who is not brought into contact with such topics is certainly not bound to think about them; if he be, he will find the absence of thought respecting them a more serious impediment to him in matters directly concerning his personal life than he may at first suppose. Now, if anyone reads Mr. Coleridge's literary life, taking him to be a great poet, and therefore able to supply the principle of his art ready made and fit for immediate use and exportation, he will, I should think, be much disappointed. I cannot discover here, more than in his political work, a system. I have lately heard that there is one, and that it has been taken whole and alive out of the works of a great German author. But I am speaking only of what I saw there myself, and I am bound to say that is escaped my notice. I seemed to see a writer, who was feeling his way into the apprehension of many questions which had puzzled me, explaining to me his own progress out of the belief that all things are dependent upon association, into the acknowledgement of something with which they are associated; into a discovery that there is a keynote to the harmony. I learnt from him, by practical illustrations, how one may enter into the spirit of a living or a departed author, without assuming to be his judge; how one may come to know what he means, without imputing to him our meanings. I learnt that beauty is neither an accidental nor an artificial thing, that it is to be sought out as something which is both in nature and in the mind of man, and which, by God's law, binds us to nature. But all this comes out in a natural experimental method, by those tests and trials in which a man may be greatly assisted by the previous successes of failures of another, just as Faraday may be assisted by Davy,[3] but which he cannot adopt from another, and which we cannot adopt from him, except by catching his spirit of investigation and applying it to new facts.

[3] Michael Faraday (1791-1867) succeeded Sir Humphry Davy (1778-1829) as Professor of Chemistry in the Royal Institution.

The *Aids to Reflection*[4] is a book of a different character from either of these, and it is one to which I feel myself under much more deep and solemn obligations. But the obligation is of the same kind. If I require a politician or a critic who has indeed worked his own way through the region in which he pretends to act as my guide, I certainly should be most dissatisfied with one who undertook to write moral and spiritual aphorisms, without proving that he was himself engaged in the conflict with an evil nature and a reluctant will, and that he had received the truths of which he would make me a partaker, not at second hand, but as the needful supports of his own being. I do not know any book which ever brought to me more clear tokens and evidences of this kind than the one of which I am speaking. I have heard it described both by admirers and objectors as one which deals with religion philosophically. In whatever sense that assertion may be true, and in a very important sense I believe it is quite true, I can testify that it was most helpful in delivering me from a number of philosophical phrases and generalizations, which I believe attach themselves to the truths of the creed, even in the minds of many who think that they receive Christianity with a most child-like spirit — most helpful in enabling me to perceive that the deepest principles of all are those which the peasant is as capable of apprehending and entering into as the schoolman. I value and love his philosophy mainly because it has led me to this discovery, and to the practical conclusion, that those who are called to the work of teaching must cultivate and exercise their understandings, in order that they may discriminate between that which is factitious and accidental, or belongs to our artificial habits of thought, and that which is fixed and eternal, which belongs to man as man, and which God will open the eyes of every humble man to perceive. I have learnt in this way the preciousness of the simple creeds of antiquity; the inward witness which a gospel of facts possesses, and which a gospel of notions must always want; how the most awful and absolute truths, which notions displace or obscure, are involved in facts, and through facts may be entertained and embraced by those who do not possess the faculty for comparing notions, and have a blessed incapacity of resting in them.

It is inevitable that the person who first applies this principle to religious questions should sometimes be involved in the ob-

---

[4] *Aids to Reflection in the formation of a manly character* (1825).

scurity from which he is seeking to deliver us. Anyone who begins the work of encountering notions and theories will himself
be accounted the greatest notionalist and theorist. To get rid of
crudities and confusions, he will sometimes be obliged to adopt
or invent a nomenclature. His rigid adherence to this will be
called pedantry; his followers repeating his words, instead of carrying the meaning of them into their studies and their life, will
deserve the charge; his enemies will have a plausible pretence for
saying that he has made simple truths complex by his way of
handling them. The *Aids to Reflection* have been exposed to all
these misfortunes. Nevertheless, I have heard them generally denounced as unintelligible by persons whom I had the greatest
difficulty in understanding, who were continually perplexing me
with hard words to which I could find nothing answering among
actual things, and with the strangest attempts to explain mysteries by those events and circumstances which were to me most
mysterious, and which as they lay nearest to me, it was most
important for my practical life that I should know the meaning
of. On the other hand, I have heard the simplest, most childlike
men and women express an almost rapturous thankfulness for
having been permitted to read this book, and so to understand
their own hearts and their Bibles, and the connexion between the
one and the other, more clearly. It is a book, I believe, which has
given offence, and will always give offence to many, not for its
theories, but for its essentially practical character. Its manly de-
nunciation of the sentimental school must be painful to many in
our day who have practically adopted the Rousseau cant, though
they have changed a little the words that express it; who praise
men for being good, though they do the most monstrously evil
acts, and account it a vulgar worship of decency to say that one
who is the slave of his own passions, and enslaves others to them,
may not be a very right and true man notwithstanding. And yet
those who do really exalt decency above inward truth and conformity to a high standard will not at all the more own Mr.
Coleridge for an ally because the school which pretends to oppose them reject him. The whole object of his book is to draw us
from the study of mere worldly and external morality to that
which concerns the heart and the inner man. But here, again, he
is so unfortunate that those who have turned "heart-religion"
into a phrase— who substitute the feelings and experiences of
their minds for the laws to which those feelings and experiences
may, if rightly used, conduct us — will be sure to regard him as

peculiarly their enemy. So that if there were no persons in the land who did not belong to one or other of these classes, if there were not many who have tried them all, and are weary of them all, it would indeed be very difficult to understand how it is that this volume has found its way into so many studies, and has gained access to so many hearts.

The idea of the first *Lay Sermon,*[5] that the Bible is the statesman's manual, is less developed, I think, than any of those to which I have alluded hitherto. But the bare announcement of it has been of more value to me than any lengthened exposition that I know of. There is no topic which has more engaged my attention in these volumes than the national history of the Bible, but I have said very little indeed of which that thought was not the germ.

The little book upon *Church and State*[6] you will suppose, from the title and character of these volumes, that I am likely to have studied still more attentively. And indeed, if you watch me closely, you will discover, I doubt not, many more thoughts which I have stolen from it than I am at all aware of, though I think I am conscious of superabundant obligations. It seems to me that the doctrine which I have endeavoured to bring out in what I have said respecting the relations between Church and State, is nothing but an expansion of Mr. Coleridge's remark respecting the opposition and necessary harmony of Law and Religion, though in this, as in many other cases, I have departed from his phraseology, and have even adopted one which he might not be inclined to sanction.

The robberies which I have confessed are such in the truest sense; they are conscious and deliberate robberies. If anyone had chanced to discover in my book twenty or thirty pages which he could trace to some English or foreign author, I should think his common sense, though he might allow no scope for charity, would induce him to hesitate before he imputed to me a wilful fraud. It is so much more likely that I should mistake what has been for years mixed with my own compositions for one of them, than that I should take such a very stupid and blundering way of earning a reputation, which a few years must destroy

[5] *The Stateman's Manual . . . A Lay Sermon addressed to the Higher Classes* of Society (1816).

[6] *On the Constitution of the Church and State, according to the idea of each . . .* (1830).

altogether, that a court of justice, on the mere ground of evidence, would be inclined, I should suppose, to take the tolerant
side. If it had any hesitation, the reason would be that an insignificant author might do many things with impunity, which a
writer of eminence, who had enemies in every direction, would
be a madman to venture upon; or else it would be from a feeling
of this kind that, if I had merely forgotten myself, I should have
had some vague wandering impression of having read a similar
passage somewhere else, and, therefore, that I should, being
honest, have at least thrown out some hint, though it might not
be exactly the right one, as to the place whence I might have
derived it, thus making my reader anxious to see what had been
said by the writer to whom I referred: if I did that, of course all
suspicion of evil design would vanish immediately from the mind
of anyone who was capable of judging, or did not industriously
pervert his judgment for the purpose of making me out to be an
offender. But the use I have made of your father's writings is of
entirely a different kind from this. I could not be convicted of it
by a mere collating of paragraphs, and, therefore, if I were anxious to conceal it, I should be really, and not apparently, dis-
honest. And this is not the less true because it is also true that
the main subject of my book is one which (so far as I know) he
has not distinctly treated of, that the thoughts which he has
scattered respecting it, though deeply interesting are not always
satisfactory to me, that I have, therefore, very commonly found
myself without his guidance, and that I have sometimes wilfully
deserted it. I shall not fulfil the purpose of this letter, if I do not
show how these two apparently opposite statements are recon-
ciled.

No man, I think, will ever be of much use to his generation,
who does not apply himself mainly to the questions which are
occupying those who belong to it. An antiquary, I daresay, leads
a much easier and quieter life than one who interferes with his
contemporaries, and takes part in their speculations. But his
quietness is his reward: those who seek another must be content
to part with it. Oftentimes, I doubt not, every man is tempted to
repose in some little nook or dell of thought, where other men
will not molest him, because he does not molest them; but those
to whom any work is assigned are soon driven, by a power which
they cannot resist, out of such retirement into the dusty highways of ordinary business and disputation. This, it seems to me,
was your father's peculiar merit and honour. The subjects to

which he addressed himself were not those to which he would have been inclined, either by his poetical or his metaphysical tendencies. But they were exactly the questions of the time; exactly those which other men were discussing in the spirit of the time. And as we who belong to a younger generation have inherited these questions, we inherit also the wisdom which dealt with them. But there are, it seems to me, questions which we have not inherited — questions which belong more expressly to us than they did to our immediate predecessors. These, I suspect, we must humbly study for ourselves, though the difference will be very great to us, whether we invent a way of investigation for ourselves, or try to walk in a path which better men who have been before us have with great labour cleared of its rubbish, and by footmarks and sign-posts have made known to us.

One of the questions to which I allude is that which your father was led, I believe by the soundest wisdom, to banish, in a great measure, from his consideration, after the events of the French Revolution had taught him the unspeakable importance of a distinct national life. I mean the question whether there be a universal society for man as man. I have stated some reasons in these volumes why I think every one in this day must be more or less consciously occupied with this inquiry; why no other topics, however important, can prevent it from taking nearly the most prominent place in our minds. There is another question belonging apparently to a different region of thought, yet I believe touching at more points than one upon this: how all thoughts, schemes, systems, speculations, may contribute their quota to some one which shall be larger and deeper than any of them. If I am indebted to your father on one account more than another, it is for showing me a way out of the dreadful vagueness and ambition which such a scheme as this involves, for leading me not merely to say, but to feel, that a knowledge of The Being is the object after which we are to strive, and that all pursuit of unity without this is the pursuit of a phantom. But at the same time I cannot help believing that there is a right meaning hid under this desire; that it will haunt us till we find what it is; that we cannot merely denounce or resist this inclination in ourselves or in others; that we shall do far more good, yea, perhaps the very good which we are meant in this age to accomplish, if we steadily apply ourselves to the consideration of it. Again, there is a question which thrusts itself before us continually, and which is the mover of more party feelings just at this time than any other,

respecting the reception of those doctrines which are expressed
in old creeds, and which concern the nature of God himself;
whether these are to be taken upon trust from the early ages, or
whether we are to look upon them as matters for our own inquiry, to be acknowledged only so far as they accord with what
seems to us either the declaration of Scripture or the verdict of
reason. In preparing for the consideration of this great subject, I
have felt, with many others, that Mr. Coleridge's help has been
invaluable to us. Nearly every thoughtful writer of the day would
have taught us that the highest truths are those which lie beyond
the limits of experience, that essential principles of the reason are
those which cannot be proved by syllogisms, that the evidence
for them is the impossibility of admitting that which does fall
under the law of experience, unless we recognize them as its
foundation; nay, the impossibility of believing that we ourselves
are, or that anything is except upon these terms. The atheism of
Hume has driven men to these blessed discoveries, and though it
was your father's honour that he asserted them to an age and a
nation which had not yet discovered the need of them, he certainly did not pretend, and no one should pretend, that he was
the first reviver or expositor of them. But the application of
these principles to theology, I believe, we owe mainly to him.
The power of perceiving that by the very law of the reason the
knowledge of God must be *given* to it; that the moment it attempts to create its Maker, it denies itself; the conviction that the
most opposite kind of unity to which Unitarianism dreams of is
necessary, if the demands of the reason are to be satisfied — I
must acknowledge that I received from him, if I would not prove
myself ungrateful to the highest Teacher, who might certainly
have chosen another instrument for communicating his mercies,
but who has been pleased in very many cases, as I know, to make
use of this one. This instruction, I say, seems to me a most
precious preparation for the inquiry which belongs more strictly
to our age, but still it is only a preparation. I cannot help feeling,
while I read the profound, and, to a theological student invaluable, hints respecting the doctrine of the Trinity, which occur in
Mr. Coleridge's writings: "This is not enough. If the reason be, as
he said it was, expressly the human faculty, belonging to rich and
poor alike — not merely those personal truths which belong to
each individual's state and condition, but this highest truth,
which he presents to us as demanding the highest efforts of
thought and abstraction, must belong to the very humblest man;

must be a sacred part of his inheritance; must in some way or other be capable of being presented to him." Anyone who has entertained this thought will find that this theological subject very soon becomes involved with the other two of which I was speaking. The hope that some day

> Wisdom may teach her lore
> In the low huts of them that toil and groan,

must wax much brighter, if we can really believe that the deepest lore is the most universal. The hope that diverse sides of thought may some day be brought into reconciliation, may begin to disconnect itself with the dreary vision of a comprehensive system, from which all life is excluded, if the central unity be that of the living Being.

Maurice, "Dedication" (from the second edition, 1842, to the Rev. Derwent Coleridge), *The Kingdom of Christ,* edited by Alec R. Vidler (1958), ii, 350 ff.

INDEX

Abbotsford, 76, 76n., 79, 86.

Accidents, *see under* outward and accidental; *see under* fancy.

Action, xiv, xvi, 40, 105—108, 113, 125; as a guide to happiness, 97n.; as energy in Cobbett, 23; as pageantry in Scott, 79, 82; feeble in Jeffrey, 11; imaginative in Shelley, 70; inhibited in Mackintosh, 94; of children, 108; atrocious in Byron, 113.

Adolphus, J. H. (editor), 59n. *A Correct, Full and Impartial Report, of the Trail of Her Majesty, Caroline, Queen Consort of Great Britain*, 59n.

Aegean Sea, 111n.

Africa, 92.

Age, *see under* epoch.

America, North, 34, 60, 126.

Anthropophagi, 115.

Antilles, 62.

Apocalypse, 111n.

Apostles, Cambridge, xin., xii, xv.

Aquinas, Thomas, 93. *Summa Totius Theologiae*, 93n.

Arabia, 4, 18, 92.

Arabian Nights' Entertainment, 85n.

Arabs, 126.

Aristocracy, 16, 23, 29, 38, 58, 60, 63, 86n., 89.

Aristole, 93. *Logic*, 93n.

Arnold, Matthew, xi.

Art, artifice in Moore, 46; inspiration, an instrument of ideal, 35; of the poet, 110; laws of, 141.

Asia, 92.

Aspasia, 73, 73n.

Association, 30, 33, 38, 96n., 108, 120, 122n., 142.

Atheism, 66.

Atheist, 68, 127; defined, 67.

Athanaeam, The, xi, xii, xviii, 1n., 6n., 12n., 22n., 31, 33n., 44n., 54n., 66n., 76n., 91n., 99n., 110n., 117n.

Athens, 86, 126.

Atlantic, 61.

Austria, 4n., 50.

Babel, xv.

Bacon, Francis, 93, 93n. *Novum Organum*, 93n.

Banim, John, 100n. *Nowlans, The*, 100, 100n.; *Peter of the Castle*, 100n.; *Tales of the O'Hara Family*, 100n.

Barrow, Isaac, 55, 55n.

Bastille, the, 34n.

Being, xiii, xiv, xvi, xviii, 25, 35, 41, 97, 110, 132, 133, 147; Eternal and Infinite, 131; foundation of human, 37; living, 149; of epochs, 4; outward in Scott, 82; poet reflects, 110; Shelley's transfigured into poetry, 70; Supreme, 66; universal, 14; the object of our striving, 147.

Bel, 115.

Benevolence, 15, 35, 64, 68, 84, 95, 97, 108, 109, 119, 123, 129, 131.

Bentham, Jeremy, 97n., 106, 117n., 121n., 122, 122n., 131, 131n., 133, 135.

Béranger, Jean Pierre, 52, 52n.

Berlin, 88.

Bible, the, 144, 145, 147.

Birkbeck College, 62n.

Blackwood's Edinburgh Magazine, 11n.

Blake, William, xxi.

Block, Andrew, 100n. *The English Novel 1740—1850 A Catalogue*, 100n.

Bohemia, 26n.

Botley, 25, 25n.

Brahmins, 126, 126n.

Brett, R. L. and A. R. Jones (editors), 51n. *Lyrical Ballads*, 51n.

Brotherhood, 14.
Brougham, Henry Peter, Baron
    Brougham and Vaux (1778–1868),
    6n., 54–65; a partisan, 58, 60;
    efforts for education, 62–64;
    energetic feeling of, 54; law reform
    of, 61; opposition to Orders in
    Council, 60; Roman Catholic
    question and, 59–60; trial of
    Queen Caroline and, 58–59;
    speeches of, 56–57, 59, 59n.,
    60–61, 61n. status among
    contemporaries, 54, 65; *Present
    State of the Law*, 61n.; *Works of
    Henry Lord Brougham*, 61n.
Bruges, 4.
Buckingham, James Silk, xii.
Buonaparte, Napoleon, 20n., 84n., 88,
    88n., 114, 135.
Burgandy, 106.
Burke, Edmund, 55, 55n., 60, 98n., 136;
    *A Philosophical Enquiry . . . the
    Sublime and the Beautiful*, 55n.;
    *Reflections on the French
    Revolution*, 98n.
Burns, Robert, 29, 29n., 52.
Butler, Joseph, 93. *Analogy of Religion*,
    93n.
Butler, Samuel, 51n. *Hudibras*, 51.
Byron, George Gordon, sixth Lord
    (1778–1824), xvii, xx, 11n., 18,
    41, 44n., 49, 49n., 110–116; as a
    poet, 116; human nature falsified
    by, 115; poetry of, 112–115; *Cain:
    a Mystery*, 115, 115n.; *Childe
    Harold*, 113, 115; *Don Juan*, 113;
    *English Bards and Scotch Re-
    viewers*, 54n.; *Vision of Judgment,
    The*, 115.

Calvinists, 18.
Cambridge, university of, xii, 63, 63n.
Campbell, Thomas, 63, 63n.
Canning, George, 60, 60n.
Capitalists, 13n., 39.
Carlyle, Thomas, 10n.
Caroline, Queen Consort of George IV,
    58n.
Carpenter, Edward, xiv n.
Catholic, Roman, 18, 26, 27, 59–60.

Catullus, 73n.
Celadons, 38.
Cervantes, Miguel de, 49, 87. *Don
    Quixote de la Mancha*, 49n., 51n.
Chalmers, Thomas, 60, 60n.
'Change, Exeter, 19, 19n.
Charles I, King of England, 17n.
Charles II, King of England, 49n.
Character, 3, 42; of a people, manifested
    in its government, 86, 123; in
    Byron's poetry, 114–115; in
    Edgeworth's writings, 101; in
    Scott's works, 80; in Southey, 15.
Chatham, William Pitt, first Earl of, 55,
    55n.
Chinese, the, 45, 126.
Christ, xiii, xiii n., 68.
Christianity, 16, 17, 67–69, 127, 143;
    all-inclusiveness of, 143; distinc-
    tions of, 69; religion in its highest
    form, 119.
Christian Socialist movement, xix, 16n.
Christus Consummator, xiii.
Chunee, the elephant, 19n.
Church, the, 12, 14, 16, 31, 62, 63n.,
    145.
Churchill, Charles, 51, 51n. *Ghost, The*,
    51n.
Cicero, 56n., 57n., 93. *De Oratore*, 56n.
Circe, 107n., 111, 111n.
Circumstance, 9n., 13, 37, 39, 53, 74,
    74n., 75, 84, 86, 87, 106, 108; *see
    under expediency*.
Civilization, 124–125.
Cobbett, William (1763–1835), xix,
    22–32; a paradox, 22–23;
    contrasted with William Gifford,
    29; distinctions of, 24, 31; feeling
    for the people, 28–29; inconsist-
    encies in, 24, 28, 31; influence of,
    25; intelligibility of, 24; mind of,
    24, 27; petty politician, 31;
    sentences of, 24; supposed attitude
    toward the *Athenaeum*, 31–32;
    sustained by democratic opinion,
    22–23. *Cottage Economy*, 31;
    *History of the Protestant Reforma-
    tion, The*, 26, 27n.; *Political
    Register, The*, 28; *Poor Man's
    Friend, The*, 28n.; *Rural Rides*,
    25n.; *Sermons*, 31, 31n.

Cole, G. D. H., 22n. *Life of William Cobbett, The*, 22n.
Coleridge, Derwent, 140n.
Coleridge, Samuel Taylor (1772–1834), xiv, xiv n., xvii, xix, 10, 10n., 11n., 18n., 33n., 35n., 37, 44n., 51n., 54n., 70, 72n., 73n., 75n., 99n., 102n., 107n., 112, 122n., 125n., 130n., 131–149. *Aids to Reflection*, 134, 142–144; *Ancient Mariner, The*, 51n., 140; *Biographia Literaria* (Literary Life), 33n., 51n., 54n., 72n., 75n., 132, 141–142. *Christabel*, 51n., 140; *On the Constitution of Church and State*, 145n.; *Collected Letters of*, 51n.; *Dejection: An Ode*, 135, 135n.; *France: An Ode*, 132n., 139n., 148; *Friend, The*, 136, 140, 140n.; *Introduction to the Tale of the Dark Ladie*, 51n., *Kubla Khan: or, A Vision in a Dream*, 73n.; *Lay Sermons*, xiv, 125n., 134, 145; *Logosophia*, 134; *Love (Genevieve)*, 51; *Table Talk*, 75n.; *William Wordsworth, To*, 132, 132n.
Commons, House of, 54, 61, 61n., 62n.
Composition, xviii, 57, 91; Cobbett's, 24; Mill's, 120-122; Southey's, 15-16, 19-20.
Condillac, Etienne Bonnot de, 127; *Traité des sensations*, 127n.
Conrad, 114;
Conscience, the, xiii, xiv, xvi, xviii, 64, 93n., 128, 133, 137n.; as consciousness, 3, 20, 118, 118n., 121, 127; as feeling, 105–107; foundation of, 117.
Conservative, 134, 140.
Constantinople, 121.
Constitution, British, 16, 20, 63, 86, 89, 101.
Copenhagen, 140.
Counterfeit, xiv, xix, 19, 45–46, 82–83, 109, 113–114, 140; *see under* evil.
Cowley, Abraham, 51, 51n.
Crabbe, George, 38.
Creator, 109.
Critic, the, xvi, xvii, 76, 112–13; Cobbett as, 28; Jeffrey as, 6–11; Maurice as, *see under* Maurice;

Southey as, 12, 16–18, 16n.
Cromwell, Oliver, 114.
Cumberland, poor of, 40.
Curtain Theatre, 77n.
Cyclops, 115.

Daglish, Eric F., 25n.
Dagon, 115.
Daniel II, 85n.
Davy, Sir Humphry, 50n., 142. *Salmonia, or Days of Fly-fishing*, 50n.
Declaration of Independence, 34n.
Deism, 129, 129n.
Deist, 127.
Deity, *see under* God.
Democracy, xx, 13n., 86.
Demosthenes, 59.
Diction, 21, 37, 55, 75, 120.
Diderot, Denis, 9, 9n.
Donna Julia, 115.

East India Company, 119n.
East, the, 4, 79.
Ebro, the, 78.
Edgeworth, Maria (1767–1849), 99–109; children's stories of, 99–100; erroneous educational system of, 108–109; fictional characters of, 101–102; literary forms of, 100; moral aims of, 100; system of, 99n., 101, 102–104. *Harry and Lucy*, 99; *Parent's Assistant, The*, 99; *Practical Education*, 99n.
Edinburgh, 76n.
Edinburgh Review, The, xvi, 6–11, 18, 33n., 54n., 91, 102n., 117n.
Education, 62–64, 81, 88n., 99n., 100, 102–109.
Egypt, 4, 67.
Eldon, John Scott, first Earl of, 45, 45n.
Elizabeth, Queen of England, 79.
Emancipation, 27n., 59–60.
Encyclopaedia Britannica, 119, 119n.
Encyclopaedia Metropolitana, xii, xiv n.
Encyclopédie, 9n., 103n.
Energy, *see under* action.
England, 26n., 33, 34, 63, 85, 130, 131, 134.

Epicurus, 106, 121n.
Epoch, an, 1n., 5, 5n., 35, 53, 79, 82, 88–89, 94–95.
Eskimo, 126.
Essay, the, xx, 19, 100; contrasted with the speech, 57.
Essayist, xx–xxi, 12, 16n., 54n., 76n., 91, 119n.
Establishment, the, *see under* church.
Etruria, 4.
Euclid, 121. *Elements*, 121.
Europe, 34, 78n., 82, 85, 88, 92, 139.
Evil, xiv, xx, 10, 19, 26, 33, 42, 47, 61, 63, 72, 84, 84n., 108, 113–115, 129, 133, 144, 146.
Exeter College, Oxford, xii.
Expediency, xvii–xviii, 9n., 74n., 91n., 96–97.

Faction, *see under* partisan.
Fancy, xix, 7, 11, 20, 33n., 44, 49, 50, 51n., 52, 53, 55, 75, 75n,. 78, 103.
Faraday, Michael, 142.
Faust, 14, 23, 56n.
Feeling(s), xvii, xix, 10, 13, 17, 23, 25, 26, 27, 28, 33, 35, 36, 37, 40, 41, 42, 43, 44, 46, 48–49, 54, 56, 64, 66, 68, 69, 70, 71, 77, 81, 82, 85, 92, 94, 95, 97, 100, 102, 103, 105, 106, 107–108, 109, 110, 113, 114, 115, 117, 128, 137, 141, 144, 147; as faith, 137; as sympathy, 29, 33, 35, 37, 38, 40, 41, 42, 46–47, 77, 85, 97, 102, 104, 113, 114, 120, 141.
Florence, 4, 48n.
Form(s) xvii, 14, 35, 42, 93.
Fox, Charles James, 60, 60n.
France, 22, 23, 35, 60n., 88, 103, 134, 136.
Frey, Albert R., 79. *Sobriquets and Nicknames*, 79n.

Ge, 25n.
Genius, xvi, 2–3, 5n., 14, 33n., 41, 70, 73, 74, 75n., 79n., 112; Coleridge's poetical, 140; compensation balance for society, 41; reforms the age, 88; flaw in Shelley's 71, 73;

master of ideal creation, 14; reformer of the age, 88; task of, to harmonize logic and sentiment, 120–121.
George III, King of England, 15n.
George IV, King of England, 22, 22n.
Germany, 4, 4n., 26n., 35, 42, 88, 136, 142.
Gifford, William, 29, 29n.
God, xiii, xiv, xv, 10, 13, 14, 17, 25, 27, 40, 62, 64, 66, 67, 67n., 68, 69, 71, 108, 111, 112, 115, 118n., 119, 122n., 125, 125n., 129, 129n., 130, 132, 133n., 134n., 137, 138, 142, 143, 147, 148.
Godwin, William, 10, 10n. *Enquiry Concerning Political Justice*, 10n.
Goethe, Johann Wolfgang, 10, 10n., 42, 56.
Good, the, xiv, xvi, xvii, xx, 11, 13, 16, 19, 31, 35, 42, 44, 53, 58, 61, 63, 64, 67, 71, 74, 81, 85, 89, 94, 96, 102, 104, 112, 122n.; defined, 67.
Government, xviii, 31n., 32, 33, 53, 86, 95, 104, 122, 136.
Gradus ad philosophiam, 75n., 122, 130n., 136n.
Granada, 4.
Grattan, Henry, 55, 55n., 56, 60.
Greece, 4, 40, 59.
Griggs, Earl Leslie, 51n.

Hades, 111.
Haidee, 115.
Hamlet, an epitome of humanity, 14.
Happiness, *see under* feeling.
Hare, J. C., 137, 138.
Harold, 114.
Harpies, 115.
Hartley, David, 131.
Hearnshaw, F. J. C., 63n. *Centennary of King's College 1828–1929, The*, 63n.
Heliodorus, 118, 118n.
Helvétius, Claude Arien, 9, 9n., 80, 80n.
Hermes, 107, 107n.
Hero, of Moore, 50; of Wordsworth, 37.
Highlands, the, 79.
Hindu, 27, 124, 126, 126n.
Hindustan, 4, 123.

History, aspects of, 5, 5n., 17, 17n., 44,
    89, 91, 96, 126; Christian
    interpretation of, xvi; Mackintosh's
    approach to, 94—95; Maurice's view
    of, *see under* Maurice; Mill does not
    understand, 124; of Coleridge's
    mind, 140; of English parliaments,
    123; Mackintosh's knowledge, 92;
    Scott's view of, 79, 81—82, 89; the
    spirit of, 125.
Hobbes, Thomas, 35n., 93, 93n.
    Leviathan, 67n., 93n.
Homer, 87. *Iliad, The*, 70, 70n.;
    Odyssey, The, 107n.
Hone, William, 19n. *Every-day Book,
    The*, 19n.
Hottentots, the, 126.
Humanity, a mockery of, 38; common,
    xix, 16, 27; condition of, 13;
    constitution of, 39; debasers of, 61;
    degradation of, 110; essential, 119;
    language, the sign and organ of, xv;
    Shelley creates a perfect specimen
    of, 74; social, 41.
Hughes, Thomas, xvn.
Hume, David, 96, 122. *Treatise on
    Human Nature*, 96n., 122n, 148.
Humour, 49, 49n., 81, 84; *see under* wit.
Huss, John, 26, 26n.
Hutchinson, Mary 51n.

Ideal, the, xx, 13.
Imagination xvii, xix, 11, 40, 66n., 91n.,
    128, 130, 140; Brougham lacking
    in, 54, 54n.; Cobbett lacking in, 25,
    25n.; Coleridge's distinction
    between fancy and, 51n.; fancy, a
    complement of, 75, 75n.; feelings
    acted on by, 33—34; Jeffrey lacking
    in, 11; Mackintosh lacking in, 98;
    Mill's system opposes, 130; of
    Ireland, 44; organ of feeling and
    thought, 25; reveals truth, 117n.;
    Shelley's, 72, 72n., Wordsworth's,
    35.
India, 122,124, 126.

Indians of North America, 126.
Inspiration, xvi, 2, 25, 35, 59, 70, 70n.,
    73; as a Power, 15; Shelley's, a

    conviction of moral good, 71;
    Wordsworth's rare, 35.
Ireland, 34, 34n., 44, 53, 85, 100, 101.
Isadas, 57, 57n.
Isocrates, 57.
Italy, 23, 35, 50, 85, 88.

Jacobins, 18.
Jacobites, 78.
Jamaica, 62.
Jeffrey, Francis Lord (1773—1830), xiii,
    xvi, xviii, xx, 33n., 74n.; and the
    Edinburgh Review, 6—11;
    anonymous editor and critic, 6—7;
    depreciations of Wordsworth, 8,
    8n.; expediency of, 8, 9, 74n.;
    limitations of, 11, 11n.; mind of,
    9—10, writings of, 8, 9—10.
Jerusalem, 25.
Jews, 134.
Joan of Arc, 127n.
Job, 28n.; book of, 127.
John, St., 111n.
Jones, A. R., 51n.
Jones, Sir William, 127.
Jonson, Ben, 77, 77n. *Everyman in his
    Humour*, 77n.
Jove, 111.

Kant, Immanuel, 96, 132, 135, 136.
    Critique of Pure Reason, 96n.
Keats, John, xvii, xx.
Kensington, 25, 25n., 32.
Keswick, 18, 18n.
Kingdom, *see under* society; *see under*
    nation.
King's College, London, xii, xix, 63n.,
    69n.

Ladurlad, 49n.
Lais, 73, 73n.
Language, abuse of, 68; cant, 36;
    Cobbett's 24; critics and fundamen-
    tal, xviii; general nature of, xiv-xxi;
    interpreter of conscience, xiv;
    Jeffrey's, 7; metaphor, 72, 72n.;
    Mill's, 120; mystical nature of, xiv;
    of Nature, 118; of oratory, 54n.,

55; of religion, 129; philosophical, 117; Scott's, 80; Shelley's, 75; Wordsworth's, 36-38, 42.

Laud, William, 17, 17n.

Law, the, Brougham divided between government and, 64; crown an emblem of, 85; Mackintosh and criminal, 95; Mackintosh and international, 98; Moore and general, 50; of art, 100; of being, despised by Byron, 113; of people, 124; of universal truth, 117.

Leibniz, Gottfried Wilhelm, 93, 93n.

Leighton, Robert, 107, 107n.

Leonardo da Vinci, 79n.

Lesbia, 73, 73n.

Lessing, Gotthold Ephraim, 10, 10n.

Liberals, 13n.

Licinian rogations, 86, 86n.

Listener, The, xvi n.

Literary Chronicle, The, xii.

Literary excellence, foundations of, 35, 125n.

Literature, xii, xiv, xv, xx, 50, 76n., 77, 80n., 87, 92, 103, 117n., 118, 123, 127; business of, 119; contemporary, 35, 92; English, 1–5; of India, 126.

Little, Thomas, *pseudonym* of Thomas Moore, 44n.

Lochaber, 85.

Locke, John, 80, 80n., 93, 122, 122n. *Essay Concerning Human Understanding*, 93n.

London, xii, University of, 62, 62n., 63, 85.

Long Island, 25, 25n.

Long Parliament, 17n.

Love, 14, 41, 67, 68, 68n., 69, 105, 108, 125, 125n.; binds sects, 27; cardinal point in Christianity, 69; cherished by great men, 107; Cobbett without the wisdom of, 31; element of genius, 14; element in God, 14; germ of, in flowers, 41; in ethics accompanies intelligence, 120; pedlars thrilled by impulses of, 38; Shelley pours good into, 72; universal, 68, 108.

Lucretius, 71n.

Ludlow, J. F. M., xix.

Luther, Martin, 26, 26n., 40.

Maccabees II, 118n.

Mackintosh, Sir James (1761–1832), 61, 91–98, 127; compositions of, 91, 98; expediency in, 96–97; mind of, 94; philosophical garment of, 93; talent of, 92–93; utilitarian, 96–97; Whig, 95; without imagination, 98. *Vindicae Gallicae*, 98.

Madame du Deffand, 53.

Madrid, 88.

Mammon, 25, 137.

Manchester Guardian Weekly, 110n.

Mankind, 25, 35, 37, 61, 61n., 62, 102, 107, 109, 114–15; *see under* people.

Marchand, L. A., xviii. *Athenaeum Mirror of Victorian Culture*, xviiin.

Mary, Queen of Scots, 79.

Maurice, Frederick Denison (1805–1872), xi-xxi *passim*, 1n., 13n., 16n., 17n., 19n., 25n.; 27n., 33n., 44n., 51n., 54n., 60n., 66n., 69n., 71n., 72n., 75n., 86n., 89n., 91n., 99n., 102n., 110n., 117n., 121n., 122n., 125n., 130n,; on Coleridge, 131–149; on literature, 1–5, 118; as critic: aims at truth, 3, 5; applies Coleridge's distinction between reason and understanding, 54n., applies Coleridge's theory of the co-presence of fancy with imagination for poetic perfection, 75n.; seeks a general impression, 112; uses the foundation of literary excellence, 35, 116n., 125; critical comments on: action, 103–108, based on conscience, experience and enlightenment, 117; Coleridge's distinction between reason and understanding, 102n.; contemporary versus traditional philosophy, 117–118; expediency as weakening morality, 97; feeling as the guide of intellect, 99n., 102.; growth of society, 86, 125n; literary history from Milton to Wordsworth, 33–35; poet as creator, 14–15,

110–111; works of imaginative
mind, 87; definitions of: atheist,
67; God, 67; happiness, 64; moral
author, 83; virtue, 64; Whig, 95.
Conscience, The, xiv n., 72n.;
Eustace Conway, xiv n.; *Friendship
of Books, The*, xvn., xvi n.;
Introduction to Hare's *Charges*,
138; *Kingdom of Christ, The*, xii,
xiii n., *Moral and Metaphysical
Philosophy*, xii, xiv n., 135, 136;
Subscription No Bondage, xv;
Theological Essays, xiv n, xvii n.,
69n.; *Tracts on Christian Socialism*,
xxi n.; *What is Revelation?*, xvi n.
Maurice, Colonel Frederick, xi n. *Life of
Frederick Denison Maurice, The*, xi
n., xiii n., xxi n.
Mechanics' Institute, 62, 62n.
Medici family, 48n.
Memory, 94.
Methodism, 12, 131.
Metropolitan Quarterly Magazine, xii.
Mexico, 18.
Milan, 88.
Milesians, 101.
Mill, James (1773–1836), 117,
119–130; compositions of,
120–122; creed of, 122; *Essay on
Government* analyzed, 125–126;
History of British India, analyzed,
122–125, 126–129; problem of
civilization in, 124–125; profes-
sional pretention of, 121; religion
of, opposed by Maurice, 128–129;
style in, 120–122. *Elements of
Political Economy, The*, 119; *Essay
on Government*, 119, 119n., 125,
126; *History of British India, The*,
119, 122, 126, 128.
Mill, John Stuart, xix n. *Autobiography*,
xix n., 121n.; *Utilitarianism*, 97n.
Milton, John, 14, 33, 34n., 36, 37, 37n.,
40, 49, 51, 51n., 55n., 75, 85, 87,
107, 112, 113n. *L'Allegro*, 49;
Areopagitica, 37; *Paradise Lost*,
55n., 85n.
Mind, the, belief at the root of, 128;
fiction exhibits, 87; of poet, a
mirror of the world, 110; of
Socrates, 107, 117; onward

movement of, 89; poetry, the
spontaneous outgrowth of a poet's,
xvii, 46; state of, resides in
consciousness, 106.
Minotaur, 114.
Monthly Review, The, 36n.
Moore, Thomas (1779–1852), xx, 8, 20,
44–53; a circumstance of the age,
53; contrasted with Wordsworth,
51; defects in poetry of, illustrated,
46–47; disguises human nature, 46;
imagery in, 45–46; *Irish Melodies*
of, 46, 47n.; poems of, deficient in
truth, 45; poet of fancy, 49, 51,
51n.; political squibs of, 51–52;
prose of, 52; pseudonyms of, 44n.,
52n. *Epicurian, The*, 52; *Fables of
the Holy Alliance, Rhymes on the
Road*, 52, 52n.; *Fudge Family in
Paris, The*, 52, 52n., *Intercepted
Letters or, The Twopenny Postbag*,
52, 52n.; *Irish Melodies*, 47n., *Lalla
Rookh, an Oriental Poem*, 52, 52n.;
Life of Sheridan, The, 53; *Little's
Poems*, 52; *Memoirs of Captain
Rock*, 52, 52n., *Where Shall we
Bury our Shame*, 50n.; *Works*, 47n.
Morality, xiv, 2, 2n., 9, 11, 14, 26, 34,
35, 61, 66, 71, 74, 75, 80, 82–84,
93, 95, 96–97, 100, 102–104,
106, 107, 112, 116, 117, 119, 125,
143, 144; words as instruments of,
xvi, xviii, 68–69.
Morgan, Lady née Sydney Owenson,
100, 100n., 101.
Morning Post, The, 51n.
Moscow, 88.
Musidoras, 38.

Nation, as an individual, xv; as a people,
1, 1n., 86, 123; experience of, 125;
essayists as mouthpieces of, xx;
soul of, xv.
Nature, a treasury of symbols, 35; Byron
no sympathy for, 112; catholic
faith in, 37; falsification of, 115;
foundation of, 37; glory of, 119;
human, 16, 17, 107, 119, 121;
Mill's system of, 122, 125; Moore
diverts from, 46, mystery of, 110,

poet purifies, 50; resources of,
applied, 118; Scott's idea of, 80;
Shelley analyzes, 71; Sibyl, 118,
118n.
Neapolitans, 50, 50n.
Negro, 126.
Neo-classic phraseology, 34, 34n.
New Testament, The, 69.
Newton, Sir Isaac, 35n.
Nineteenth Century, The, 70n.
Novel, the, 30, 78n., 80, 88, 100, 102.

Old Testament, The, 48n., 127.
Olympus, 111, 111n.
Opie, Amelia, 36n. *Warrior's Return,
The*, 36n.
Orders in Council, 60.
Oxford, xii.
Outward, the, 11, 26, 42, 45, 64, 74, 78,
79, 93, 113, 117, 125; *see under*
accidents; *see under* fancy.

Pallas, 107.
Pan, 30.
Pantheism, 128, 128n., 129.
Pantisocracy, 135.
Paradise, 25.
Paris, 88, 126.
Partisan, 16, 18, 27, 58, 60, 92, 95, 102;
as faction, xix, 12, 16, 25, 26, 27;
as sect, 13, 16, 27, 39, 42, 58, 104.
Party, Conservative, 134, 140; *Edin-
burgh* (6–11), *Quarterly*, and
Westminster as organs of, 117n.
Pascal, Blaise, 103; *Pensées*, 103.
Patmos, 111.
Patriot, the Swiss, 106, 106n.
Peace Society, the, xii.
Peel, Sir Robert, 61.
Peninsular War, 20.
People, Brougham's need to rely on, 60;
Cobbett's feeling for, 28; growth
of, organic, 125, 125n.; Mackin-
tosh, no leader of, 94; mind of,
realised in institutions, 123, 126;
redemption of, through action of
heroes, 106; Scott opposed to, 86;
see under humanity.
Perfection, Supreme, 68.

Pericles, 73n.
Pestalozzi, Johann Heinrich, 107, 107n.
Philosophes, 103n.
Phyllis and Chloe, 73, 73n.
Plato, xviii, 20, 93, 107, 127, 132.
Platonism, Christian, xii.
Plunket, William Conyngham, first
Baron, 60, 60n.
*Poetical Register and Repositary of
Fugitive Poetry*, 36n.
Poet, xvii, xix, xx, 12, 14, 16, 44, 51,
51n., 66, 72, 72n., 110–111, 116;
Byron, second-rate, 116; geniune,
125n.; holy task of, xvi, 50–51;
laureate, 12n., 18, 20; masters of
the generation, 2–3, 14; mind of,
110–111; Moore, second-rate, 51;
romantic, xvii; Shelley, imaginative,
70, 75, reformer, 71; Southey,
second-rate, 15; Wordsworth,
inspired, glorious, 35–36, 38,
40–41, 42.
Poetry, artificial between Milton and
Wordsworth, 33–34, 34n.; as
action, 40; Byron's, 113–115;
Moore's, 44–52; muse of Shelley's,
prophetic, 73; not a pretty pastime,
111; of Wordsworth and Shelley,
xvii; Shelley's being, transfigured
into, 70; Southey's, 15–16, 21;
spontaneous outgrowth of mind,
46; Wordsworth's, 38, 40, 41.
Poland, 78n.
Politics, 16–17, 23, 29, 31, 34, 53, 63,
85, 95–96, 117n., 123, 125, 134,
136.
Poor, *see under* people.
Pope Alexander, 51.
Popedom, the, 26.
Power, all-informing, 68; of periodical
essayists, xviii.
Priestley, Joseph, 131, 131n., 133; *Essay
on the First Principles of Government*, 131n.
Principles, xviii, 24, 34, 43, 44, 53, 58,
67, 68, 69, 81, 92, 94, 96–97, 102,
108, 110, 114, 130, 134, 136, 142,
143, 148.
Prophet, Ezekiel, 68, 111; Isaiah, 111,
127; Mohammed, 26, 121n.; nature
as, 118n.; poet as, xix, 73, 111n.

Protestant, 26, 27.
Provençal, 53.
Providence, xviii, 17, 20; *see under* God.
Prussia, 1n., 126.

Quarterly Review, The, xvi, 16, 20, 29n., 76n., 117n.

Raphael, 23.
Reason, xiv, xviii, 33, 54, 54n., 68, 91n., 95, 96n., 99n., 102, 102n., 110, 122n., 130, 130n., 136; essential principles of, 148; wondrous in Shelley, 72.
Reconciliation, xiv, 25n., 129, 149.
Reekie, 76.
Reformation, 7, 26, 28n., 88, 138.
Reform Bill, xvi, 23n.
Religion, coincidence with will and reason, xiv; expression of human being, xviii; law and, 145.
Reviewers, xviii, xx, *Edinburgh*, 6—11, 11n., 18, 22, 76n., 91, 117n.
Revolution, French, 7, 34, 88n., 89, 91n., 98n., 131, 135, 136n., 147.
Ricardo, David, 122, 122n.; *Principles of Political Economy and Taxation*, 122n.
Richardson, Alan, xvi n.
Robinson, Mary, 36n. *Poetical Works*, 36n.
Rochester, John Wilmot, second Earl of, 49, 49n.
Roman Catholic, 18, 26, 27, 59.
Romance, 52n., 76, 87, 100n., 114; Scott confuses history with, 88.
Romanticism, xix; miraculous descent on English literature, 35; wondrous regeneration, 5.
Romilly, Sir Samuel, 61.
Rousseau, Jean Jacques, 9n., 144.

Sanskrit, 127, 127n.
Satan, 18, 85n., 113n.
Satire, 19, 51—52, 130.
Schelling, Friedrich Wilhelm Joseph von, 135.
Schiller, Johann Christoph Friedrich, 87.

Scotch *feelosofers*, 25, 31, 32.
Scott, Sir Walter (1771—1832), xiii, xvi, 10n., 11n., 20, 50n., 76—90, 106n.,; approach to history, 79, 81—82, 88—89; barren psychology of, 80; benevolence of, 84; characters of, lacking in will-power, 83; compositions of, 87—88; confuses history and romance, 88; defects in writings of, 79—81; descriptions in, 78, 80, 81—82, 87; observer, 76; outward look of, 76, 78, 82; political opinions of, 85—86; spell-monger, 76; wizard of the north, 79n.; wretched idea of man, 80. *Antiquary, The*, 87; *Battle of Sempach, The*, 106n.; *Bride of Lammermoor, The*, 87; *Heart of Mid-Lothian, The*, 87; *Life of Napoleon, The*, 88; *Old Morality*, 87; *Waverley*, 78, 78n.
Scylla, 114.
Sect, *see under* partisan.
Selfishness, an age of, 84; calculative philosophy leads to, 108; expediency leads to, 97; Scott opposed, 84; Shelley opposed, 68, 69; Wordsworth corrected, 40.
Sentence, the, of Brougham, 56—57, 59; of Cobbett, 24—25; of Mill, 120—122; of Moore, 48—50, 52—3; of Southey, 19; *See under* composition, style, words.
Serena, 49n.
Shaftesbury, Anthony Ashley Cooper, third Earl of, 93, 93n.
Shakespeare, William, xvi, 14, 37, 42, 48, 49, 77, 77n., 79, 80, 87, 116. *Macbeth*, 79n.; *Othello*, 115.
Shawcross, J. (editor), 33n. *Bibographia Literaria*, 33n., 51n., 54n., 55n., 72n.
Shelley, Percy Bysshe (1792—1832), xv, xvii, xviii, xix, 37, 66, 66n., 68—75, 83—84, 84n., 129n.; builds another creation, 71; errors in opinions of, 72—73; faults in poetry of, 73; fancy in, complements imagination, 75, 75n.; fundamentally poetical, 70; human embodiment of Imagination, 70, 72, 72n.;

inculcates perfectibility, 74; not
   anatheist, 68; opposes philosophy
   of circumstance, 74; social
   reformer, 71; teaches love to God
   and man, 69. *Julian and Maddalo*,
   83, 84n.; *Ode to the West Wind*, xv;
   Queen Mab, 68; *Stanzas Written in
   Dejection*, 71n.
Sheridan, Richard Brinsley, 49, 49n.
   Rivals, The, 49n.; *School for
   Scandal, The*, 49n.
Simmons, Jack, 13n., 18n. *Southey*,
   13n., 18n.
Smith Elsie, 11n., 36n. *An Estimate of
   William Wordsworth by his
   Contemporaries 1793—1822*, 11n.,
   36n.
Smith, Sydney, 6n.
Society, 13—14, 23, 29, 38—40, 41, 71;
   as a kingdom, xiii—xv, xviii, xix; for
   the Diffusion of Useful Knowledge,
   6n., 62.
Socrates, 107, 117.
Solon, 86.
Sophist, the, 9.
Southey, Robert (1774—1843), xvi, xix,
   11n., 12—21, 28n., 49n.; biographer, 19; controversialist, 19;
   decline of vision in, 16—18; defects
   of, 19—20; early idealism of,
   13—14; interpretation of history in,
   17; mode of composition, 15,
   19—21; poet, second-class, 14, 15;
   poetry of, 15—16, 21; politician,
   16—18. *Book of the Church, The*,
   16; *Curse of Kehama, The*, 15, 49n;
   History of The Peninsular War, The,
   16; *Life of Nelson, The*, 19;
   Roderick, the Last of the Goths,
   15; *Sir Thomas Moore: or
   Colloquies on the Progress and
   Prospects of Society*, 19; *Tale of
   Paraguay, A*, 15; *Thalaba, The
   Destroyer*, 15; *Vision of Judge-
   ment, A*, 15.
Spain, 20n., 23, 50, 78n., 85.
Spartans, 56.
Spenser, Edmund, 14, 37. *Faerie
   Queene, The*, 37, 111.
Spinoza, Benedict Baruch, de, 132.
Stebbing, Henry, xi n.

Sterling, John, xii.
Stilicho, Flavius, Roman Emperor, 49,
   49n.
St. John, the apostle, 111n.
Stoa, 126.
Strafford, Thomas Wentworth, first Earl
   of, 17, 17n.
Style, logical in Mill, 120—122; of
   Brougham, 55—57; of Mackintosh,
   91, 98; of Moore, 50, 52; of
   Southey, 20; *See under* sentence,
   words.
Systems(s), 13, 19—20, 21, 135n., 141,
   149; Benthamite in Edgeworth,
   99n., 101, 102—3, 106, 108;
   Brougham's educational, 63—64;
   contemporary English social, 39,
   62, 130; Edgeworth's moral, 108;
   hardening of, 133—134; Hindu
   social, 123; Mackintosh makes, 94;
   Mill's judicial, 125; none in
   Coleridge, 134—135, 142.

Tchudi, the minstrel, 106n.
Tennyson, Alfred Lord, 70n.
Thomas Brown the Younger, *pseudonym*
   of Thomas Moore, 52n.
Thoulouse, 4.
Thucydides, 86n.
Titan, 25, 25n.
Tories, 6, 16n., 17n., 28n., 60n., 76n.
Transcendentalist, 135.
Trench, Richard Chenevix, xv.
Trevelyan, George Macaulay, 22n.
   English Social History, 22n.
Truth, xix, 14, 23, 25, 27, 35, 41, 45,
   65, 67, 68, 81, 92, 96, 98, 102n.,
   107, 109, 113, 117n., 120, 130,
   137, 143, 148; Byron, no love of,
   112; poet, interprets universal, 111;
   the business of literature, 119, 125,
   125n.
Turkey, 85.
Tweed, 76n.

Uffizi gallery, 48n.
Understanding, the, 54n., 94, 99n., 102,
   102n., 122n., 130n., 136, 143.
Ulysses, 111, 111n.

Unitarians, 18, 131, 131n., 133, 139, 148.
United States, 60n.
Unity, xv, 16n., 27n., 39n., 40, 70, 132, 138, 138n., 147, 149; of feeling in Shelley's poetry, xvii, 70; spirit of, in Wordsworth, 38.
Uranus, 25n.
Utility, 96; philosophy of, 121, 121n., Utilitarians, 97, 97n., 135.

Vandals, the, 48.
Vedas, the, 126n.
Venus, 48.
Versification in Shelley, 75.
Vesta, 49, 49n.
Vidler, Alec R. xiiin.
Vienna, 88.
Villiers, 79.
Virgil, 89n. *Georgics*, 89n.
Vistula, 78.
Voltaire, François Marie Arouet de, 1, 1n., 9, 9n., 49, 127; *La Pucelle*, 127, 127n.

Waterloo, xvi.
Wellington, Arthur Wellesley, first Duke of, 20n., 24.
West India, slavery in, 61.
Westminster Abbey, 110n.
Westminister Review, The, 117n.
Whatley, Richard, 121n. *Logic*, 121n.; *Rhetoric*, 121n.
Wheatley, Henry B., 19n. *London Past and Present*, 19n.
Whig, 18, 95.
Whitmore, Charles Shapland, xii, xiin.
Wickliffe, John, 26, 26n.
Wilkins, Sir Charles, 127n.
Will, the, 61, 74, 83, 103, 133, 134, 135n., 143; coincidence with reason and religion, xiv, xviii.
Winkelried, Arnold von, 106n.
Wisdom, Essential, 68.
Wit, 11, 20, 49, 51, 52, 55, 103.
Word, the, xiv, xxi, xxi n.; Incarnate, xvi.
Words, xv, xvii, xviii, 21, 56, 68, 106, 118, 124, 144.

Wordsworth, William (1770–1850), xiii, xvii, xviii, xix, 10, 11n., 14, 20, 29n., 30n., 33–43, 51, 70, 91n., 112, 129n., 132n.; aims of, 35, 38; a philosophical Christian, 43; clamour against, 36; Coleridge interested in, 33n.; compared with Shakespeare, 37; concerned with the purport of existence, 35; contemporary publications of, 36, 36n. contrasted with Goethe, 42; corrects narrowness of feeling, 40; criticism of, 8, 8n., 33n., 36n., defects of, 38, 41–42; diction compared with that of Coleridge and Shelley, 37; first great imaginative poet since Milton, 33–34, 34n.; individuality of, 41; influence extended, 36; inspiration of, 35; mind of, 39–42; nature, a treasury of symbols for, 35, 40–41; Preface of, 37n.; teaches universal harmony, 39; Poetry of: diction in, 37; heroes in, 37; imagery and language of, 37, 42–43; imaginative forms in, 35; universality of, 38. *Ecclesiastical Sonnets*, 37n., *Excursion, The*, 14, 37, 51; *Lyrical Ballads*, 8n., 29n., 51n., 99n.; *Peter Bell*, 30, 30n., 36n.; *Poems in Two Volumes*, 8n., 36n.; *Poetical Works of*, 36, 36n.; *Prelude, The*, 91n.; *River Duddon Series, The*, 11n., 37n.; *She Was a Phantom of Delight*, 51; *White Doe of Rylstone, The*, 37.

Yamen, 49n.
Yeats, William Butler, 44n.

DATE DUE

Demco, Inc. 38-293